MICHE

M000202493

Navigating the Friendship Maze

The Search for Authentic Friendship

MICHELE HOWE

Navigating the Friendship Maze

The Search for Authentic Friendship

HENDRICKSON PUBLISHERS

Navigating the Friendship Maze: The Search for Authentic Friendship

© 2018 Michele Howe

Hendrickson Publishers Marketing, LLC
P. O. Box 3473
Peabody, Massachusetts 01961-3473
www.hendrickson.com

ISBN 978-1-68307-138-9

Printed in the United States of America

First Printing—May 2018

Library of Congress Cataloging-in-Publication Data

A catalog record for this title is available from the Library of Congress
Hendrickson Publishers Marketing, LLC ISBN 978-1-68307-138-9

To Eunice

A spiritual mom to many
A faithful friend to all

Contents

Acknowledgments

I think it is most appropriate, given the topic of my latest book is friendship, that I offer my sincerest, most heartfelt, and humble thanks to everyone at Hendrickson Publishers for treating me like a friend of their family. Beginning with the illustrious editorial director, Patricia Anders, whose extraordinary skill at editing and refining my work is unparalleled. I also am so pleased to have the ongoing pleasure of working with Meg Rusick, Maggie Swofford, Phil Frank, and Tina Donohue. Each of these individuals is highly talented, and they worked in perfect synchronization to put together and create the book you now hold in your hands. Cue enthusiastic applause on their behalf now! May the Lord bless each of you. I'm reminded of what Paul says in Colossians 3:23–24, that those who do God's work get God's pay. My hope is that our heavenly Father rewards each of you beyond your expectations. Thank you once again for helping this author's dream come true.

I also want to thank Les Stobbe, my longtime agent and friend, who is my go-to guy whenever I have questions. I'm blessed to know you.

Introduction

*T*he irony of God's timing never ceases to amaze me. I've been mulling over the importance of women's friendships for years now. I started to picture in my mind's eye what friendship would look like if it were displayed like a hand-drawn etching laid out flat on a large table. The shape that immediately leapt to my mind was that of a maze. I could see a full page of partially intersecting pathways that looked promising at the outset but were actually dead ends. Other paths went up and down and all around and just seemed frustrating to follow. Still others took sharp turns and zigzagged back again before progressing ahead. Then there was a path that, although you had to look ahead before committing yourself to move forward, became clearer that this singular road was the right one with each step. A lot like real life friendships, right?

We may begin a friendship only to have it end abruptly. Another friendship may take us on an emotional roller-coaster ride where we feel uneasy and off-kilter most of the time. Others may take us nowhere fast and neither friend seems to mature and grow. And then there's the path to biblical friendship where we are sensitive to God's leading, we understand the high stakes of commitment involved, and we quite happily begin the journey of life together confident that our friendship is a God-honoring, authentic one.

The book you hold in your hands is the product of the maze I described above. I'm excited to share with you *Navigating the Friendship Maze: The Path to Authentic Relationships*, presented in three sections that I hope will guide you through the ins and outs of biblical friendship. We'll discuss first the definition of biblical friendship and why a biblical friendship is essential, as opposed to a more casual one. Next, we will explore the various types of friends every woman needs in her life. Did you realize you need different types of friends? You do, and so do I! Finally, we dive into ten practical ways to be a friend who stays committed and stays the distance.

Back to my opening statement about the irony of God's timing in our lives. When I began writing this book, I was going through what I would call my lonely-stretch season. One of my best friends moved to another city. Another friend was hectically busy caring for her elderly, dying father while juggling work and weekly babysitting commitments for her grandchildren. Another friend's adult daughter, husband, and three grandchildren moved back into their family home while her daughter's house was being built and as her daughter was undergoing cancer treatments. Still another friend had spent much of the past five months traveling to another state to assist her daughter, who had just given birth to premature twin girls. For my part, I had been exhausted from the spring season and was so looking forward to a lazy, hazy summer reprieve. Instead of relishing the sun, beach, and the promise of three months to replenish my energy supply, the summer was overrun with work, repairs, travel, more work, and still more house repairs.

During that summer, my friends and I tried to squeeze in a couple of hours here or there to just chat and catch up, but it never happened. For some crazy reason, every time I was free my friends were not and vice versa. After weeks of scheduling nightmares, I decided to step back and concentrate on my work, my family, and my responsibilities and be thankful for the long-distance communication we shared as friends. I kept being reminded that here I was writing a book on the importance of having good, solid female friends who consistently build into one's life and I was enduring a season without much contact from mine.

I had to laugh at the irony. Over time, as I sat down at my computer and labored over each chapter, I realized more keenly than ever how powerful biblical friendships are and how they impact our lives for good. With every chapter I worked on, I felt the subtle sting of missing my friends' presence more and more. I realized afresh how much I need my friends' wise words, encouragement, inspiration, laughter, perspectives, and yes, even their gentle words of correction. I honestly believe that God allowed me to be set apart, alone and lonely, all through the summer months, so that he could remind me of all the ways he intends for friendships to bless our lives.

It is now well into the fall season as I write this, and I'm thankful to report that I've been able to spend some much needed time with several of my friends and have scheduled more coffee dates in the coming weeks. I hope that as you, dear reader, work through these thirty chapters on learning the here-and-now importance (as well as the eternal repercussions) of navigating the friendship maze with wisdom, insight, and relational savvy, that God will bless you deeply. We all need someone (or a few someones) to walk alongside us through life's sometimes treacherous, wearisome paths. Here's to biblical friendships and all that they do to enrich our lives for God's glory and our good!

Part One

Defining Biblical Friendships (Why They Are Essential)

Chapter 1

Let's Define Friendship in General

A friend loves at all times.

Proverbs 17:17a

Older women, younger women, women who are
peers—we all need each other if we are to adorn
the gospel and show its beauty in our lives.

Nancy DeMoss Wolgemuth

On certain days, a painful distant memory sometimes makes its way to the forefront of my mind. I remember the moment with perfect clarity. My husband and I were standing in our dining room speaking to a young police officer who came to interview us after we alerted the authorities that our then twenty-year-old daughter was missing. I was crying. Of course, I was crying. I was wondering if we would ever find our daughter or if I would be numbered among those tragic mothers whose child was lost or taken, never to know where or why. During that heartbreaking conversation, the back door to our kitchen opened and my friend of over fifty years walked in. I hadn't asked her to come. I hadn't told her that I needed her support. She knew it without my asking. We hugged each other, and then I resumed the conversation with the police officer. My friend didn't say a lot. She didn't need to. Her glistening eyes said more to me than any amount of words ever could. She was telling me that she was there with me. She supported me. She was with me all the way—wherever and whatever that meant. The police officer wrote down all the information we could give him about our daughter, and then he drove away in search of my precious lost child. My friend stayed, and her presence that afternoon only confirmed what I already knew: I had a friend who would help me face this day and every day thereafter.

Thankfully, the ending to this life-altering, horrific day ended well when my daughter came home hours later, uninjured but still unrepentant and rebellious. Though we thanked God (and the officers who went looking for her), my husband and I knew we had a long journey ahead of us with our child. I also recognized something else. I realized I would need some good friends to support me through the coming months as we tried to untangle the mess of my daughter's life. My friend's caring presence that day reminded me that I wouldn't have to look far for support. That's what a friend is for. Today. Tomorrow. Always.

Many women will never have to face the situation I just described above. They will, however, endure their own trials, tribulations, challenges, and unthinkable life events. How do I know this? Because we live in a sin-ridden, broken world and heartache comes to us all. It simply arrives in different sizes, shapes, and levels of intensity. I'm also sure that all women need a few good friends to love them, listen to them, pray for them, and journey with them through it all. Real friends, the kind we all need, stick around for the duration. Authentic friends are present in the dreariest days of fall, the bitter cold of winter, the tumultuous changeableness of spring, as well as the happy, sun-filled days of summer.

Besides being defined by Webster's Dictionary as a noun, *friendship* has many other synonyms: benevolence, brotherhood, charity, cordiality, fellowship, goodwill, kindliness, and neighborliness. If you study these words, you get the picture that it's all good. A real friend is one who wants what is best for you and is willing to sacrifice herself for your benefit.

Of course, every woman needs different kinds of friends too. In the following chapters, we'll discuss the various types of friends every woman must cultivate throughout her life and why. We'll also look at what it means to become an authentic friend through God's enabling grace and power.

 Take-away Action Thought

When a friend of mine is in need, I will stop and ask God to direct me in the specific ways I can be of help.

My Heart's Cry to You, O Lord

Father, I want to thank you for placing faithful friends in my life at every season. Help me to be mindful that not everyone has been blessed by the friendships of godly women. When there is opportunity to love and serve a friend, give me your wisdom and your insights on how to be a tangible blessing to her. Show me what is needed in the moment according to the circumstance and the situation. If I cannot find the right words to speak, let my presence demonstrate how much I love my friend. Even in those moments when I'm not able to be physically present, remind me that I can spend time faithfully interceding on my friend's behalf. Thank you, Lord, for the gift of friendship. Help me to keep growing into the kind of friend you want me to be. Amen.

Focus on Friendship

1. Look for ways to connect or reconnect with longtime friends (or brand-new friends) through e-mail, phone calls, or texts. Make her day by reminding your friend what she means to you.
2. Be sensitive to the ever-changing dynamics of friendship and keep current with the challenges/struggles your friend may be facing.
3. Pray for your friends every day, and ask the Lord for opportunities to love them in practical ways.

 # Chapter 2

Why Biblical Friendships Are Essential

She speaks with wisdom,
and faithful instruction is on her tongue.
Proverbs 31:26

*Sound doctrine is radically transformational. Lived
out, it changes everything about us. It counsels us. It
corrects us. It's like an onboard guidance system,
directing and determining our course. And ultimately
it transforms the culture through us and around us.*

Nancy DeMoss Wolgemuth

Most individuals glide right through their outpatient surgery experiences with minor pain and few complications. Some thirteen years ago, immediately following my first of six shoulder surgeries, I would have told you I had that very same positive experience. Six weeks later, however, I felt completely the opposite. After more than six weeks of sleepless nights compounded by two years of almost constant caregiving and excessive stress, my body was weary, weakened, and worn out. It quickly became a season of trying to gain back my physical, mental, and emotional strength day by day. I was keenly reminded that in some very real ways our bodies run like machines and they can break down through overuse or abuse. I had admittedly pushed myself to my limit, no longer able to handle everything life (and people) was throwing at me. I thought I could do it all. I was wrong.

I called this my dark season of the soul. When your body and your emotions are in upheaval, your spiritual well-being is likely in a similar place—in need of healing. I remember one afternoon in particular, I was crying out to the Lord when a longtime friend stopped by unannounced. Her first words to me were, "When I got up this morning, I felt like a magnet was pulling me up here to see you." I cried.

As my friend and I sat on my living room couch talking about my surgery and how awful it was to not sleep, she pulled out her Bible and read some comforting verses to me. Today, I cannot tell you the passages she shared, but I can tell you that her presence and her reading Scripture to me helped me immensely. What I treasured and needed most of all was someone who loved me enough to sit with me, listen to me, and then gently redirect my faulty thinking back toward God and what he has to say in the Bible. My friend was kind, patient, and gentle. She was also a warrior on my behalf who challenged me to rely on Jesus, my ultimate healer. Because I was confident in my friend's stalwart love for me, I was able to gain some emotional and spiritual momentum toward long-term healing that afternoon. She spoke biblical truth into my heart and it stuck. Every woman needs a friend like that, and every one of us needs to be that friend for another woman.

That afternoon so many years ago is just one of many instances I can happily recall when a godly, Christ-honoring friend met me wherever I was and in whatever state I was in, acting like an iron-sharpening-iron companion who cared about me. It's important for us to grasp the difference between a so-called friend who is happy to visit when we are feeling under the weather or need to talk versus the biblical friendship model God calls every one of us Christ followers to emulate. Certainly, my dear friend was genuinely happy to come visit me when I was feeling so undone and listen to my heart. The distinction is that my friend wasn't willing to leave me in my suffering without providing God's healing balm of powerful promises. The difference here is that one friend is happy to offer some lightweight comfort while the other leaves you with biblical truth to meditate on, continues to pray for you, and checks in on you long after others have forgotten your pain and struggle.

Christ followers must determine to be the type of friend the Bible describes. We lend our hearts and our hands and whatever resources we possess to lovingly serve our friends (and others), but we don't stop there. Christian women who have studied the Bible understand that it should continually challenge, teach, and transform us—while we in turn continually seek to challenge, teach, and allow God's redemptive and purifying work to transform our friends. It is not enough to simply dip in and out of a friend's life when they are going through a crisis. Rather, each of us needs to study the word of God to show ourselves approved (ready and able) to pass on his life-giving truths to those we call friends. Biblical friendship never leaves a friend wondering where to find the Living Water. Biblical friendship seeks to communicate the power and active nature of the promises found in the Bible so that these truths will change lives forever. Biblical friendship is the very definition of unconditional love: it always protects, always trusts, always hopes, and always perseveres (1 Corinthians 13:7).

 ## Take-away Action Thought

Whenever I am trying to encourage a friend who is hurting, I will share a living word of hope with her before we part.

My Heart's Cry to You, O Lord

Father, help me to see the importance of looking at every problem, every pain, from an eternal perspective. Give me the needed wisdom for each situation I encounter so I can truly minister your good word of hope to my friend. I never want to stop short of sharing how you may be working in my friend's life, even during the hardest seasons of suffering. Help me to be gentle, kind, and compassionate. Give me ears to hear what my friend is telling me. When all her words have ceased, enable me to offer your life-giving perspective. Show me how to impart lasting hope and the path to joy, despite the pain my friend is suffering. Above all, give me the words to speak that will spark a desire in my dear friend's heart to honor you by trusting you in her most desperate moments. Amen.

Focus on Friendship

1. Beginning today, dedicate some specific time to studying the Bible and locating verses that describe the attributes of a godly friend.

2. This week, write down a selection of these verses and meditate on them throughout the day.

3. Once you gain a more thorough understanding of how God defines friendship, ask the Lord to reveal to you the areas where you are weakest and then seek to overcome them.

 *Chapter 3*

We Become Like Those We Associate with Most

Walk with the wise and become wise,
for a companion of fools suffers harm.

Proverbs 13:20

How do you live an authentic life with God? It always starts with the truth. Telling the truth to Christ saves us, right there in the middle of our mess. It exposes who we really are and allows our authentic selves—our darkest secrets, shames, and shadows—to be redeemed.

Sheila Walsh

When I was in high school, I chose a friend who affected me greatly. Or should I say she chose me to great negative effect? In either case, I heard this small warning bell go off in my head at the very outset of our friendship. Even though I had become a Christian when I was twelve, I had no clue what it meant to be a Christ follower. So, clueless me passively accepted this girl's friendship and we started going to football games, hockey games, and other high school events. She was smart as a whip and talented too.

The problem was that the words on her tongue were sharp: she was always disparaging someone else, and she also used foul language. To my memory, I had never spoken a curse word in my life until I became friends with this girl who could swear using words I didn't even know.

You can guess what eventually happened. After some months of casually hanging around her, I started swearing too. Not to the extent that my friend did, but I recall using one word in particular whenever anything went wrong. Then I realized I was changing in ways I didn't like. Looking back, I know it was the still, small voice of the Holy Spirit cautioning me, teaching me, and challenging me to make a change. I started considering other ways this girl was negatively influencing me by mere association. I don't remember ever making conscious choices to use a curse word or talk about others critically or take on such a pessimistic attitude toward life in general before she entered my life. But eventually I did. Soon after graduation, I began to distance myself from this friend until one day I realized we weren't (and never had been) true friends.

I remember this negative relationship whenever a new person enters my friendship zone. It's always stuck with me that, though I might be careful in choosing a new friend, I need to have the right motives when doing so. The quotation above by Sheila Walsh is right on the mark. We need to ask ourselves why we want this particular person for a friend. If we don't, we could end up so altered as time goes on that we may not recognize ourselves. We have to tell ourselves and others the truth and learn to be authentic women no matter who we are with.

Over the years I've been observing this principle cited in the book of Proverbs: "Walk with the wise and become wise, for a companion of fools suffers harm." Everywhere I look, I see the same pattern. Groups of female friends who spend lots of time together begin to mirror one another. They seem to do so unconsciously. Friends who hang out a good deal of the time together enjoy the same activities, have lots in common, and may even start to look alike as they alter their clothing and hairstyle choices. It's almost like osmosis. But it can be so damaging—to us and to our friends.

Recently, I was part of a group of diverse women who met together periodically to discuss book topics. Over time, I started to see this principle in action once again. Each of the women in the group had their own inner circle of close friends. Within these smaller sub-circles, the women who had a natural affinity for one another spent generous amounts of time together. Over the months, I began to see that they were starting to take on each other's mannerisms, attitudes, and even mirroring each other's way of thinking.

While I would guess that none of them was aware of how much their tight-knit group was influencing change in their individual lives, I as an outsider could see it. I took this observation further and realized as we sat discussing the struggles we were having in our lives that these sub-groups never rose above (in attitude or action) their fellow group of friends. I believe their closeness and the way they viewed their faith walk was so similar that none of them challenged any of the others to grow, nor were they accountable to each other. This shocked me at first. Then I realized how much sense it made. When our closest friends fail to keep us accountable as sisters in Christ, we often don't grow in our faith or our character. Since we become like those we spend the most time with, we need to navigate the friendship maze wisely.

Take-away Action Thought

I must prayerfully take the time to consider and pray about my current friendships and how my life, my choices, my words, and my attitude affect them as well as how they affect me.

My Heart's Cry to You, O Lord

Father, the longer I walk with you, the more I recognize the immense impact friends can have on one another. I continually see friends who are caught in sin and struggle and how their friends are mired right along with them. I believe with all my heart that I need to take a careful, prayerful look at every relationship I am a part of to make sure I am walking with women who place honoring you in the highest position of their lives. In all ways, I want to know you, Lord, and make you known. Let this attitude shine brightly through me and through my friends. Amen.

Focus on Friendship

1. Each season, take some time and prayerfully consider the friendships in your life. Objectively ask yourself if honoring God is the highest priority for you and your respective friends.

2. Considering that most women have several friend clusters in their lives, consciously invest in your friends' spiritual growth by asking them specific questions and dialoguing with them about the Lord.

3. If you find yourself in a group of friends who are pulling you away from the Lord and your love for him, either attempt to redirect the direction of the group or opt to leave it.

 # Chapter 4

Influenced or Influencing?

The prudent see danger and take refuge,
but the simple keep going and pay the penalty.

Proverbs 22:3

*The humble . . . are keenly aware of their dependence
on God in all areas of life, suspicious of their sinful
hearts, very mindful of the dangers they face, and
diligent to avoid stepping into sin's trap.*

Lou Priolo

I was sensibly aware of the friends my four children made during their elementary, middle-school, and high-school years (and beyond). As a mom, I was always deeply conscious that even the most casual conversations and interactions they had with their friends would affect them. It's not that I tried to listen in on them as they played, talked, or even worked on their homework together, but my mom radar was set on "high" all the time. I don't believe this was a bad thing. In fact, as a mother and now a grandmother, I am convinced God gave me that internal warning system to help guide and protect my children from harm—and in this case, relational harm.

While every child (and adult) lapses at times and gives us reason to pause about the wisdom of the relationship, I'm not talking about small insignificant character flaws. Rather, as a mother who understood the power wielded by intimate friendships to make or break the formation of godly character, I was watchful. I realized that all daily the instruction and training that my husband and I had invested into our children's lives could be undone by a single ungodly friend.

With this principle at the forefront of my heart and mind, I remember the day when I discovered that a "good" friend of one of my daughters had stolen money from my daughter's bedroom. I talked at length with my child about the situation, and she was clearly as upset as I was. Not only did her so-called friend steal from her, but also my daughter's heart was broken that someone she trusted would do that to her. On so many levels, that singular scenario hit hard, and I learned a lot in the ensuing days about how to (and how not to) handle sticky situations with the parents of my children's friends.

After I approached this girl's mother, the money was returned. But the interaction I had with this mother was nothing less than unsettling. When I carefully and kindly explained the situation, she was brusque and cold toward me. Yes, she told me she would "get to the bottom of it," which apparently she did because her daughter brought the money back to our home later that afternoon. I didn't, however, see any indication that the girl's mother felt remorse or even concern about her child's behavior. It was almost as if she had been through this so many times before that she was numb to the poor choices her elementary-aged daughter was making. This mother's response made me all the more decisive in severing the friendship. I realized that something bigger than her friend's attitude and actions was influencing my child. There was a whole family of influencers I had to contend with who seemed to think little of godly character qualities such as honesty, trust, and loyalty. We cared too much about our young daughter's forming character than to let this situation undermine what we were attempting to teach our child.

Influenced or influencing? The humble of heart recognize that each of us is susceptible to being permanently altered and changed by the subtle or not so subtle influence of others. Though we'd like to believe that a friend's unhealthy, unwise, or even sinful choices will not affect us, we're wrong. As Proverbs 22:3 states, "The prudent see danger and take refuge, but the simple keep going and pay the penalty." As adults, we like to believe that we are smarter, savvier, world-wise, and far too experienced to fall into the traps a friend may be mired in. But we are not. No matter what we may think, our decisions regarding life in general and choosing friends in particular must be sifted through the lens of God's word.

As I look back on my daughter's painful experience with her friend, I remember frequently questioning her about whether or not she was being influenced by her friend or if was she doing the influencing? Of course, my daughter, who loved her little friend, said she was making sure they were obeying our family rules and not sneaking around behind our backs trying to get away with things they knew were dishonest. I didn't fully believe it because over time I started to see small but significant attitude changes in my daughter. I knew my child intimately, and I could see that she was being influenced by her friend's attitudes and actions. I've never forgotten how hard it was to communicate our concern and love for our daughter's character and well-being as we told her we wanted to her stop spending time with this friend. There were tears, protests, pleas, bargaining, and then outright anger. It was hard on us, on our daughter, and on this other child. Looking back, I now realize I should have been more diligent at the outset of this budding friendship than I was. After that painful scenario, I took future steps to be sure I was more attentive at the beginning of any or all friendships. It all comes back to these two simple questions: Are you the influencer, or are you the one being influenced?

 *Take-away Action Thought*

I will purposely ask the Lord to reveal to me whether or not I am being the influencer or if I am being influenced by my friends.

My Heart's Cry to You, O Lord

Father, I know I sometimes struggle to believe that a friend's poor choices will ever impact my life, but you know that they do. Whether my friend's attitude and actions are subtle or life altering, they do change me. I may not recognize any differences in my heart and mind at first, but over time how my friend chooses to lead her life will affect me. Give me the good sense and your godly wisdom to pull back from those who hinder me from honoring you in every area of my life. Help me to use the influence I have to gently redirect my friend back to the saving faith found only in you and to your word of truth. Clothe me with a spirit of humility. Help me to recognize the slyness and subtlety of secret sin and expose it. Thank you for protecting me in every area of my life. Amen.

Focus on Friendship

1. Today, make a list of your friends and ask the two questions: Are you the influencer? Or are you being influenced? Once you have worked through this friendship list, prayerfully ask the Lord to reveal if any of your friendships are hindering your relationship with him.

2. If you believe you are in a friendship that is directing you away from God, find a gentle way to ease away from spending so much time with this friend.

3. Make a list of practical steps you can take to influence your friends toward trusting Christ and living a God-honoring life before him. Through prayer, e-mail, text, or phone call reminders, share God's promises with your friends to encourage them to follow after him and not grow discouraged.

 *Chapter 5*

Frenemies or Friends?

Wounds from a friend can be trusted,
but an enemy multiplies kisses.
Proverbs 27:6

*Real relationships are messy. They inevitably bring a share
of pigeon droppings. Sometimes you are the one who feels
dumped on—and other times, you're the pigeon doing the
dumping, and someone else, literally, feels the impact.*

Paula Rinehart

S ome years ago I was painfully reminded of a statement
that speaker Paul Tripp made about friendships in general: "People will tell you who they are. You just have
to pay attention." Tripp explained that as we observe how individuals treat those already deeply enmeshed in their lives,
we will have the insight to know how they will eventually treat
us. Tripp believes (and I agree) that there aren't exceptions to
this rule. People will reveal their truest character over time
by how they act and interact with others. Give anyone enough
time and they will show you who they really are on the inside.

A mistake often made by well-meaning individuals is that they believe if they tread cautiously, carefully, and avoid their friend's hot-button topic of choice, then they will be the single exception to Tripp's rule of thumb. Unfortunately, this isn't so. In moments of tension or stress, people will react to you just as they react to others. This type of "magical thinking" of being able to opt out of a friend's poor behavior toward you simply because you are trying so hard to be a good friend won't work long term. I learned this hard truth firsthand.

I remember a woman taking the initiative to befriend me after we casually ran into each other over a period of months. Soon afterward, she told me I was one of her closest friends, which I thought odd since we hardly knew each other. Not too much time had elapsed before this woman began telling me how she was handling conflict in other relationships. It wasn't pretty. I remember feeling rather shocked by how she described her reactions toward others who said something or did (or didn't do) something that angered her. It was scary.

At that point, I realized I could very well be the next casualty in her long line of friendships gone bad. I was right. All it took to end our friendship was a brief e-mail in which she misunderstood my intentions and told me so. From there on out, it didn't matter how I tried to overcome the obvious coldness and dislike she now had for me personally; we were no longer friends. Then she began to slander me to others, which took the situation to an entirely new level. I remembered Paul Tripp's warning and replayed it over again in my mind for months as I dealt with trying to heal from her harsh (and to my mind, needless) rejection. A friend who treats others poorly will in time do the same to you.

In the first chapter of this book, we defined what friendship looks like. Then we studied the difference between casual friendships and biblically based ones. Now, let's explore the concept of "frenemies," which is a clever term for those who masquerade as friends but whose actions reveal themselves to be enemies. Sometimes, frenemies don't expose themselves for a long while. For others, it doesn't take long for these sorry souls to privately and publicly derail and undermine you at the every possible turn. How do you learn to recognize a frenemy?

I believe a wise place to begin is to look at the overall relational patterns in a friend's life. Do they make friends and keep them? Or do they make friends and lose them just as quickly? Do they evidence genuine care and concern for others, or do they seem consumed with caring only about what benefits them? How do they handle conflict? Do they stick around long enough to work it out, or do they bolt? When there is an issue between themselves and others, do they verbally crucify the other person or give them grace?

Frenemies quietly masquerade as your potential next best friend, so be wise and take Tripp's recommendation seriously. Be alert to the ways your friends choose to handle disagreements, disturbances, misunderstandings, and other "messy" relational elements. Although messiness is a part of all relationships that go the distance, conflicts between friends should never end the relationship. Rather, they should strengthen it.

Take-away Action Thought

I will watch for any signs that my acquaintances and new friends are not able or willing to put effort into working through the difficult stretches that come along in every friendship.

My Heart's Cry to You, O Lord

Father, open my eyes to see relational danger when it is staring me in the face. Help me to not ignore the Holy Spirit's warning in my heart. I know that every friendship, every relationship, has its shares of growing pains and struggles during some seasons of life. I don't want to shy away from the hard work of maintaining a good friendship, but I do need your wisdom when seeking out new friendships or when others seek mine. Make me a wise woman who carefully guards her steps. Above all, never allow me to take on the role of being a frenemy to my friends. Grant me your strength and grace to give all I have for their well-being. Amen.

Focus on Friendship

1. Pray to become a wise woman who recognizes the signs of an unhealthy friend who mistreats those in her life. Be cautious before you casually enter into a friendship with a woman who cares only about herself.

2. If you are in a relationship where it is clear that you're being treated as a frenemy and not a true friend, pray for the right words and the most effective way to speak to your friend about your concerns.

3. If you're suffering from the fallout of a frenemy's attacks, ask God to help you fully forgive, pray for this former friend, and even bless her. Pray that you will be set free from any possible bonds of lingering anger or bitterness.

 *Chapter 6*

What to Look for in a Real Friend

Let your eyes look straight ahead;
fix your gaze directly before you.

Proverbs 4:25

I want to live lavishly the life that God has set
before me, trusting his glory to peek through
the torn edges. I want to go for broke.

Paula Rinehart

I was facing a personal crisis of sorts. I knew what I should do, but I also knew what I felt was the easier road. No one would have condemned me if I had chosen to take the path of least resistance. But I continued to wrestle hard with my decision. Night after night, I woke up troubled as the deadline loomed closer, alternately fluctuating between anxiety (if I said yes) and regret (if I said no). Finally, I asked for the advice of two of my friends. I met with each friend alone, shared my dilemma, and asked for their counsel. One friend told me to forget about the more difficult (for me) option. She asked me why I would even consider it given the choice could mean more work, extra time commitment, and some uncomfortable risks. My friend, whom I am confident wanted only the best for me, gave me plenty of legitimate reasons for begging off from this particular opportunity.

Then I met with another friend and her advice was completely the opposite. She pointedly began asking me specific questions about why I was hesitant to say yes. What in my heart was cautioning me from moving forward? What was motivating me? In what part did I see the supernatural working of God enabling me to execute this task? Was I holding back because I believed I was ill-equipped or not talented enough? After we worked through these introspective questions and dialogued back and forth, I recognized that I was hesitant to say yes because I was afraid of making mistakes, worrying I wouldn't succeed, and nervous about taking the risk. My dear friend gently chided me for spending too much time thinking about "me" rather than trusting that God could work through me.

After those two conversations, I went home and prayed. To be honest, it didn't take long for me to decide to go for the riskier option. After talking the situation through with my second friend, I realized I would be sinning by not saying yes. God presented this opportunity to me, and he knew I needed him and his abiding strength and grace to complete the task, but I had to trust him enough to take that first step. As I look back on those two quite opposing words of advice, I realized that one friend banked her all on God's faithfulness to supply what I needed, while the other friend relied on what she believed I could humanly handle. Once I recognized the difference between these two perspectives, I was challenged and changed.

Because I know my own sad propensity to worry and nurture fear, I've always been drawn to people who radiate fearlessness and boldness and who are die-hard risk takers. I've been blessed to have a few of these kinds of big-dreaming, go-for-broke types of friends in my life (I've given birth to four of them too)—the kind of woman who sees God as our understanding Savior and Lord who is the all-powerful Creator and sovereign sustainer of life itself. My friends who have been willing to obey God in their own lives and follow wherever he leads them inspire me to hone this same type of spiritual strength in my life.

The women who inspire me the most have been those who invest considerable time and effort seeking God. They understand that they need to know who their God is before they can take those courageous steps of faith he asks of them. My friends study the Scriptures, make notes of the insights they glean, memorize and meditate on key passages, and pray for wisdom and insight; they also sit silently, contemplating the very nature of God. In short, they prepare for battle every single day. I've learned that the fearlessness, boldness, and risk-taking propensity doesn't come overnight. These types of Christian-warrior characteristics are developed day after day, week after week, month after month, and year after year. Real change comes with great effort. It comes slow, but it does come.

All of us need at least one friend who will exhort us to follow wholeheartedly after God. Each of us needs a friend who will challenge us to take God at his word and believe that what he promises in Scripture to do for us he will indeed do.

 *Take-away Action Thought*

I will spend time studying the attributes of God so I will be fearless, bold, and willing to take risks when God opens new doors.

My Heart's Cry to You, O Lord

Father, I want to be a fearless and bold risk-taker for you. Help me to spend the time I need to know you. Reveal yourself to me every day and equip me to serve you in every capacity you open up for me. I pray that I will not give way to worry or fear of failure. Help me to lean fully on you and your abiding strength and grace. Give me a big-picture perspective about life. Open up my heart and my mind to possibilities I may have never considered before. Bring friends into my life who will challenge me to take faith-driven steps and who are willing to talk me through whatever fears I may be harboring. Amen.

Focus on Friendship

1. When God opens up a new door of opportunity for you, spend time praying and meditating on the greatness of God before you answer.

2. Ask for prayer from women you know who have studied God's word and who know him to be the supplier of everything we need.

3. When you feel afraid of entering into a new area of work/ministry/responsibility, ask the women you know, whose life choices you respect and admire, for their candid advice on how you might overcome your struggle with fear.

Chapter 7

Warning Signs and Red Flags

If you falter in times of trouble,
how small is your strength!
Proverbs 24:10

*Think of what God has given to help us navigate relationships
in a fallen world. He has given us his Word, which is rich
in wise principles. He has given us his Spirit, who convicts
us when we are wrong, empowers us to seek forgiveness, and
enables us to show compassion to those who have wronged
us. He has given us a community of fellow Christians
where we receive ongoing correction and encouragement.*

Tim Lane and Paul Tripp

*T*hink back to a time when you failed in something that
mattered—mattered to you and to those your mistake
affected. Let's not waste time reflecting on our daily
(hourly!) minor struggles against sin that make us lean on the
Lord to break a bad habit, such as eating too much ice cream
or hitting the snooze button instead of getting up early to walk
before work. Rather, consider a time you still wince about when
you recall how you blew it. While we are forgiven of sin once we

confess it to the Lord, the fallout can continue to trouble us for years depending on the situation and our response in owning our part in the whole scenario.

Have you focused in on a single memory that you'd love to go back in time and have the chance at a redo? I have. Many years ago, I felt I had been taken advantage of and wronged over a period of months. As I struggled to cope with the mounting pressure and stress of a situation I could not remove myself from, I felt undone. I was distracted and dismayed, unhappy and lacking in peace. I asked the Lord to remove me from the situation, but that never happened. I asked him for wisdom, understanding, and grace to overcome my feelings of betrayal toward this person who (from my perspective) was intentionally harming me. I tried hard to never speak about it—thinking that the more I talked, the more upset I would become. This observation was partly true.

On a particularly weary afternoon, I was with someone I thought was a good friend and told her about the entire dismal situation. After I spilled out my heart, I momentarily felt better because I assumed my friend would offer me words of encouragement, hope, and instruction. What I received in the way of advice was just the opposite. She became angry on my behalf, applauded my sense of feeling victimized, and encouraged me to find a way to get back at this other person. In my already vulnerable state, that was the last bit of advice I needed. This wasn't biblical counsel. Not one bit.

I didn't want my friend to coddle me in my pity party, play up the numerous ways I had been hurt, and then proceed to lay out a plan of revenge! Everything about my friend's response was polar opposite to Jesus' instruction to forgive, pray for, and bless those who wrong us. I learned a hard lesson that afternoon. Not all friends have the capacity to steer us toward God-honoring decisions. If I had ever internalized any red flags about my friendship with this woman before this fateful conservation, I had no doubts afterward. Looking back, I had been in error as much as my friend who had offered me poor advice. I should have been far more conscious of her tendency to take offense, blow up, and then react in kind whenever she felt slighted. There had been ample warnings and red flags waving. I just hadn't heeded them.

Warnings and red flags are everywhere, especially in those potentially messy relational minefields. The most important warning I believe we can heed is the ability to recognize un-biblical advice as opposed to how God directs us in Scripture. There is only one path to becoming biblically literate in order to discern good advice from bad. Each of us must study his word for ourselves, daily drinking in his precepts and principles so we can show ourselves to be wise and competent Bible students. If we have friends who lack in their understanding and knowl-edge of the truths found in the Bible, then we should make it our aim to study it together.

The entire book of Proverbs exists to teach, instruct, warn, and direct us in godly living. Even if we are brand new to the Christian faith, we can read a chapter from Proverbs on our own each day. We can choose one verse a day and make it our own by copying it out and carrying it with us through the next twenty-four hours. Day by day, if we take these two steps to be better equipped for the wisdom of daily living, then we'll be able to live a wise life that honors God, correcting and encour-aging fellow believers.

Take-away Action Thought

I will take great care in prayerfully deciding to ask a friend for advice by being sensitive to how she handles her own sticky relational situations with others.

My Heart's Cry to You, O Lord

Father, help me to be discerning when I am in an emotionally weary and vulnerable place. I know that my defenses may be down and I won't always be able to catch what may be ungodly or poor advice from a friend. Give me your wisdom, your insight, and help me to be sensitive to the Holy Spirit's nudging. Show me clearly which friends are equipped to give me the biblical counsel I seek. I realize that if I choose the wrong person to talk with about my struggles, I will end up feeling worse off than if I had kept my troubles to myself. Bad advice is far worse than no advice. Help me to go first to you before I even consider confiding in others. Amen.

Focus on Friendship

1. Prayerfully go to the Lord before you seek out a friend to confide in, and study his word so you are equipped to recognize sound biblical advice from unbiblical advice.
2. Seek counsel only from those friends who have learned to obey God's word for themselves and who are intent on exhorting others to do the same.
3. If you are on the receiving end of unbiblical advice from a well-meaning friend, gently redirect and correct your friend's poor counsel.

 # Chapter 8

Biblical Friendships Add, Never Detract

The words of the reckless pierce like swords,
but the tongue of the wise brings healing.
Proverbs 12:18

How do you deal with relational disappointments?
Do you blame, deny, run away, avoid, threaten, and
manipulate? Or do you speak the truth, exhibit patience,
approach people gently, ask for and grant forgiveness,
overlook minor offenses, encourage and honor others?
Tim Lane and Paul Tripp

*I*f you have ever been in a friendship where after any interaction you have felt diminished, discouraged, or defeated,
then you need to rethink that relationship. As the title of
this chapter indicates, our friendships should never detract
from the spiritual, emotional, mental, or physical well-being of
our lives. Rather, biblical friendships should add to all of the
above. I have experienced both types of friendships over the
years and learned some hard-won lessons through both kinds.

Way back when in my early adult years, I had a friend—a
so-called friend—who did her level best to take me down with

her words. She did it so subtly that it took me a few years to realize what was happening. Not surprisingly, it wasn't even me who recognized how much of a negative impact this young woman was having on me. It was another friend who spotted telltale inconsistencies, emotional manipulation, and carefully concealed criticism. I knew how I felt after I spent time with this woman. Not good enough. Not smart enough. Not talented enough. Not successful enough. Not enough of anything.

After I'd been beaten around verbally for long enough, I finally wised up enough to place much-needed distance between myself and this other woman. When I finally set up boundaries, however, she lost interest in our friendship altogether. I could only conclude that if I wasn't compliant enough for her, she wasn't interested in an equitable friendship.

On the flip side during this same season of my life, I had another friend who inspired me, challenged me, exhorted me, encouraged me, forgave me, and was compassionate with me. She literally filled my life with good. From her positive and possibilities-driven outlook on life, to her selfless example in serving me (and others), I was determined to grow into that kind of woman (and friend) myself. Unlike the other one, this friend added to my life; although I no longer see her, the fruit of her life still blesses me.

Are you the type of friend who consistently adds to the goodness of your friends? Do you make it your life's goal to love your friends with Jesus' model as your example? Are you willing to love sacrificially, selflessly, and generously? Do you work through disagreements and disappointments? Do you ask for forgiveness and forgive others? Do you intentionally look for ways to bless your friends' lives? Are you willing to revisit the truest definition of biblical love found in 1 Corinthians 13 and develop these patterns in your life? If you are, then you are the add-on friend every woman longs for in this fallen, fickle world of temporary relationships.

On the other hand, did the story above spark any kind of conviction in your heart? Do you often take out your personal frustrations about life or about yourself on your friends? Are you more concerned with how your friends can bless you than the other way around? Do you ever consider the burdens your friends are bearing, or do you solely concentrate on your own needs? Are you willing to work through the struggles that happen in every relationship? Are you someone who gets angry and stays that way? Do you cut friends out of your life if they do or say something that displeases you? If you find yourself saying yes to any of these questions, may I kindly suggest you find a mature, trusted godly woman to help you work through your struggles? Or perhaps a biblical counselor might be the answer for more in-depth, long-held patterns of hurt. In either case, seek out help in the body of Christ. The first step to wholeness and healing is taking that first step.

Take-away Action Thought

I need to inquire of myself and honestly assess whether I am an add-on type of friend or a detract-from friend.

My Heart's Cry to You, O Lord

Father, I come to you in earnest and need you to speak plain truth to my heart. Am I the kind of friend that adds on goodness and love in all the ways that are most important to my friends? Or do I fall into the detract-from category? Am I allowing old wounds and disappointment from the past to negatively color my friendships? Help me to see the truth and to make changes where needed. I want to be the friend who consistently blesses, encourages, lifts up, and loves my friends. Even when we experience seasons when a misunderstanding may take place and our feelings get hurt, I want to work through the problems, not avoid them. Give me your grace, strength, and wisdom to rightly navigate through the often-changing waters of friendship. Help me to love my friends as I desire to be loved by them. Amen.

Focus on Friendship

1. Spend time reflecting on last year and how you handled any disappointments or disagreements that arose with your friends. If you mishandled any situation, go to your friend, ask for forgiveness, and purpose to do better in the future.

2. Reflect on the practical ways you have tried to be an add-on friend in the past year. What specifically have you done to bring good into your friends' lives? How can you do more?

3. Today, make a fresh list of loving ways, both verbal and practical, to encourage each of your friends. Specifically, find ways to highlight the strengths and talents that each of your friends possess and communicate to them how you see God using them for the good of others.

 *Chapter 9*

Knowing When to Let a Friendship Go

Fools give full vent to their rage,
but the wise bring calm in the end.

Proverbs 29:11

*When you are feeling overwhelmed by your inability to cope
with the pain you feel, when your mind is being badgered
with clever comebacks you wish you could use on your
offender, cast your cares upon the Lord. Turn your weakness
into prayer. Throw yourself fully on the grace of God, and
trust Him to handle this in His own way, in His own time.*

Nancy Leigh DeMoss

Unfortunately, all of us can most likely recall friendships that have gone terribly wrong. I think about a friend who felt betrayed when her sister started a campaign to turn my friend's teenage daughter against her and was successful for some years. I remember another woman who took sides against her lifelong best friend in favor of a fickle yet popular group of new female acquaintances at her workplace. Then there was the church split that left two former women's ministry leaders on opposing sides. All of these severed friendships were immensely painful and seemingly impossible to recover from emotionally.

Personally, I've experienced a season or two when I wondered if a friendship would ever again be repaired enough for me to regard it as a healthy one. I'm sure every woman has experienced the eventual ups and downs that long-term friendships necessarily endure, because over time both parties in a friendship have their own individual ups and downs. I know there have been specific times when I haven't been the friend I should have been. I was either so mired in my own pressing family business that I didn't have the time or energy to reach out, or I was so emotionally spent that I had nothing left to offer anyone else.

But the topic of this chapter is of a different sort than riding the waves of change with a friend. Here we are wrestling with the momentous decision of severing ties with a former friend. If you've never had to make this type of difficult and heartbreaking decision, count yourself blessed. In interviewing women across the country on the topic of female friendships, I found that most face this life-altering choice at least once in their lifetime. But how does one determine whether or not it's time to make a clean break? How can a woman be sure she is making a God-honoring decision? Read on for some foundational principles found throughout Scripture.

Given that there are myriad situations, relational dynamics, and two unique perspectives in every scenario, the only tried and true basis for making wise choices is found in the unerring word of God. So, if you believe you have come to an impasse of sorts with a friend and you have already attempted to work through the disagreement biblically, then it may be time to dissolve the relationship—at least for the present. This means that you have gone to your friend and communicated your concerns in a biblically appropriate manner—such as getting counsel from a pastor or a wise female mentor for their input and perspective, praying with and for your friend before you enter into any direct conversation, and allowing some time for private contemplation while your emotions settle. If none of this has worked, then it may be time to part ways with your former friend.

Over the years when I have found myself on opposing sides of an issue I'm especially passionate about, I've asked myself if this is an issue over which I'm willing to let a friendship die. In other words, is this impasse/offense/stance so important to me that I cannot compromise what I believe is right accord-ing to scriptural principles and not my personal preferences? This is not a simple question. In fact, I don't believe I've ever reached the place where I stopped trying to find a way to break through an impasse.

Another slice of this emotionally charged pie is the simple truth that not everyone with whom you have a disagreement will want to work through the problem. Honestly, some folks would rather fight against you (or with you) than do the hard work of battling through difficult conversations (and injured emotions) to reach a peaceable solution. Of course, facing this type of die-hard stubbornness in a former friend is yet another layer of potential pain to work through and heal from. Then there's the whole issue of working through forgiveness once the friend-ship is over. Again, diving deep into the word of God to glean everything you can on the necessity of making forgiveness your personal priority is key. Sure, over time the emotional sting may lose some of its power to hurt you, but you will be free only after you intentionally place your former friend and her offenses on the altar and then choose to forgive. There isn't any other option for the woman who desires to honor God with her relationships. And who wouldn't want God in her corner, strongly supporting her efforts to work through heartrending betrayal by seeking him and obeying his commands to forgive her enemy? Better to face the worst head-on and start the healing process than let it simmer in the backdrop of your life, always ready to erupt whenever you are reminded of the injury you felt.

 ## Take-away Action Thought

If I reach an impasse with a friend we cannot work through on our own, then I will seek out a wise, mature Christian friend or a biblical counselor to help sort the situation out.

My Heart's Cry to You, O Lord

Father, I am at a loss as to what steps to take to work out this painful situation I am facing with my friend. I am stinging because of what has transpired between us. I lay awake at night, revisiting the entire scenario in my mind over and over again. I honestly do not know what else I can do to make peace with my friend. I have prayed. I have received godly advice from my pastoral staff. I have tried to talk with her about this important issue. Nothing is working. Help me to be willing to let this relationship go if we cannot find a path of mutual respect and understanding. It hurts me to realize that this friend may no longer be a part of my life. Give me your wisdom and grace to clearly hear what I should do, and then give me the strength to obey. Amen.

Focus on Friendship

1. When you are at an impasse with a friend, don't talk about the problem with others; go directly to your friend and try to work out your differences.

2. When you and your friend can't seem to reach a peaceable solution to your problem, suggest you meet with a pastor or a biblical counselor to try and see the issue from each other's perspective.

3. If nothing works to settle the differences you both face, then prayerfully seek the Lord to understand if this impasse is worth ending your friendship over. Is it important enough according to biblical principles that you stand firm in your position?

 *Chapter 10*

Two Principles for Every Friendship

Let love and faithfulness never leave you;
bind them around your neck,
write them on the tablet of your heart.
Then you will win favor and a good name
in the sight of God and man.

Proverbs 3:3–4

*A good gardener will do what it takes to help a vine
bear fruit. What fruit does God want? Love, joy, peace,
patience, kindness, goodness, faithfulness, gentleness, and
self-control. These are the fruits of the Spirit. And this is
what God longs to see in us. And like a careful gardener,
he will clip and cut away anything that interferes.*

Max Lucado

*I*f you read carefully the Scripture passage above, you'll
note the emphasis on making love and faithfulness a foundation for your life. The quotation by Max Lucado above
also talks about the type of fruit God desires for every Christ
follower to grow and develop in her life. Notice how Lucado
finishes his thought with the astute observation that God will,

like a careful gardener, continue to clip and cut away anything
that interferes with bearing good fruit in our lives. What may
be implied, though not expressly stated, is that God can use
our friends in the role of master gardeners in our lives.

I've shared that God has blessed me with friends courageous enough to lovingly rebuke me and send me straight back
to God's word for my marching orders. What I haven't yet shared
is that the first time a good friend actually had the boldness to
offer me biblical correction, I was rather put out. The truth is
that I'd never had a peer correct me from a biblical standpoint
before. I still remember the moment it happened, many years
ago. I was at my friend's house doing some sort of craft work
with her, and I offhandedly made a comment about one of my
family members that wasn't complimentary. My friend stopped
what she was doing and gently but quite thoroughly gave me
a lesson in the importance of using every word to encourage
and build others up. She was 100 percent spot on and right
to take me to task for my careless words. I apologized quickly
and left soon after.

I'd like to say that I swiftly forgot our painful (to me) interaction but I didn't. I kept thinking about how awful I felt (and
embarrassed), because honestly I knew better than to say what
I did. It wasn't until we met again for more craft work that we
talked about the incident. By then, I was sincerely grateful
for my friend's oh-so-loving intervention of sorts. She loved
me. She wanted me to reflect Christ in every way possible. So
she did what a loving and faithful friend does: she kindly but
straightforwardly drew attention to my sin and helped me be
free of it. That's a real friend.

On that day and on many other successive days with different friends, I've been in the position my friend was in: that
of a gentle voice of rebuke to a friend. I've also been in places
where friends have had to "rescue" me. Thankfully, these re-

lationships are iron-sharpening-iron friendships. They always need to be. They always will be.

There is a second principle for friendship I believe women need to embrace for their own sakes and that of their friends. We all have different friends who serve different purposes in our lives. I have a couple of friends whom I only see when we dine out with our respective spouses. We rarely see one another outside of that particular setting. It's not that we wouldn't enjoy friendship together without our spouses; it's just been our habit to meet as a foursome. Then I have other friends whom I see only during the day. Our schedules make it much simpler to meet in the daytime when our families are at work and school. I can't even recall a time when I've seen these women after dark! Still other friends I visit with only at church and at church functions. Again, it isn't for want of trying; we just all have pressing responsibilities and leisure time has to be scheduled in advance.

Like me, I'm sure you probably have different friends for different slices of your life. There are fun friends we call when we want to laugh and kick back for a few hours, mentor friends for godly counsel and direction, ministry friends when volunteer opportunities arise, family friends we don't see other than at holidays, and vacation friends for when we go on a women's retreat or a girls' getaway. The point being that there are different friends for different parts of life. It is unrealistic to expect a single friend to meet the entire gamut of your friendship needs. Never put undo pressure on any one friend, expecting her to fulfill all your varied desires in every area of life. Friends are not a one-stop shop. Rather, variety is the spice of life in the friendship garden.

Take-away Action Thought

I will spend some time considering what type of friend I am to my friends. Am I the iron-sharpens-iron type of biblical friend God expects me to be? Do my friends fulfill that important role in my life?

My Heart's Cry to You, O Lord

Father, I am keenly aware of how I am sometimes lazy in fulfilling the biblical role of a godly friend in my closest friendships. I aspire to be the woman who has a garden full of love and faithfulness, and who blesses her friends in both word and deed. Help me to focus on developing godly character qualities and the fruit of the Spirit to be the kind of friend my friends need. Help me to have a humble and teachable spirit so that when my friends see something amiss in my attitude or actions, they feel comfortable confronting me. Help us to be reasonable with one another as well. I never want to place undo pressure on any of my friends to take on a role for my benefit that isn't their responsibility. Show me day by day what it means to be a real friend, and then help me live out those precepts in a practical way. Amen.

Focus on Friendship

1. This week, spend some time introspectively thinking and praying about whether or not you are the type of iron-sharpening-iron friend God desires you to be.
2. With careful intent, make it your mission to hone and develop the fruits of the Spirit and to let love and

faithfulness be the watchwords of your commitment to each of your friends.

3. Don't demand or become frustrated with any of your friends if they feel they have to say no to a suggestion or an idea of yours. Instead, purpose to be thankful for your friendship with no expectations on your part.

Part Two

The Kind of Friend
Every Woman Needs

 *Chapter 11*

Older, Wiser Mentor Friends

Blessed are those who find wisdom,
those who gain understanding,
for she is more profitable than silver
and yields better returns than gold.

Proverbs 3:13–14

*Lord, lay some soul upon my heart and
love that soul through me.*

Leon Tucker

f I had one piece of advice to offer a woman who is feeling
downhearted, defeated, discouraged, and even depressed
about life in general and her own life in particular, I would
tell her (as someone once told me) to look for a woman who
has traveled the road of life longer than she. I would advise her
to keep looking until God brings an older, wiser, mentor-type
friend into her life. And then never let her go.

When I was a young wife and mom, the church where we
were members started a ministry where older women were
paired with women around my age. The church staff did a
wonderful job matching women who had similar backgrounds,

interests, and even personalities. I don't recall any woman involved in this ministry who was unhappy with her ministry partner. For my part, I was matched up with a woman who could have been my mother. She was married and had grown children and grandchildren. Newly retired, she had the time and the energy to meet with me every couple of weeks at her home.

When we got together, we usually had coffee or tea and some kind of simple snack. We always spent some time working through a book we were reading together. We prayed together too. Sometimes, we tackled hands-on projects together or we made Christmas gifts in her kitchen. She taught me how to quilt, though I've forgotten most of her instruction by now. Over the weeks and months, we became friends and our friendship lasted until she moved away to another state. My friend and I tried to stay in touch, but over the years as her health failed we drifted apart. I'm confident, however, that she continued to pray for me until she passed away as I did for her.

What impacted me most about this particular friendship was that I had in my mentor friend a person to whom I could always pose spiritual, emotional, marital, and parenting questions. I recall oftentimes jotting down my questions so I would be sure to ask her about them when we next met. Her insights were invaluable to me, because I knew her past and how she had overcome so much in her early adult years. Even though we were some twenty-five years apart in age, she served as my go-to gal whenever I questioned God, struggled through an impasse in my marriage, or tried to parent effectively. When I reflect back on those interactions with her, I realize how God orchestrated our meetings, blessed them, and used them to equip me to mentor younger women.

Every woman needs a mentor friend—the type of friend described above. If you are of that certain age to be the Titus 2 older woman in a younger woman's life, please do so. Talk with your church's women's ministry leader or your pastor and start the conversation to get a ministry going in your church home. Even for those younger women who have been brought up in Christian homes with Christian parents, they still need other voices of counsel and wisdom speaking into their lives. It doesn't matter what your particular background is either. If you are actively spending time in the Scriptures, praying, meditating on God's word, and using your gifts to build up the body of Christ, then why not reach out and touch the lives of younger women?

Even if you are a newer believer to the Christian faith, don't discount the life experience and wisdom you have gained through simply having lived longer. You may not be able to spin off specific Bible verses as an answer to a younger woman's questions, but you can locate them at a later time and then revisit the conversation. You may not feel qualified to be a mentor because of your past mistakes, but God has forgiven you and wants to use your hard-won life knowledge to help other women avoid your pain. You may not feel competent to pray eloquently, but if you know Jesus as your Savior, then you can talk to him in prayer with a beautiful earnestness and spirit of thankful humility. Never allow what you deem your "weaknesses" to hinder you from obeying God when he nudges you to lovingly interact and encourage a younger woman.

Take-away Action Thought

If I am an older woman, I will search out a younger woman to mentor. If I am a younger woman, I will begin looking for an older woman to mentor me.

My Heart's Cry to You, O Lord

Father, I realize that no matter how young or old I am, you want me to spend time with women who will challenge me, encourage me, and love me. Help me to not resist your gentle nudges toward a friendship you want me to invest in. Make me sensitive to the voice of the Holy Spirit when he speaks to my heart. I pray that every woman I know finds the right friend to mentor her through the ups and downs of this life. Make us wise, humble, caring, and compassionate women as we age. Help us to gladly reach out and offer a helping hand, a word of encouragement, and the commitment to pray for every younger woman we meet. Lord, your word tells us the importance of developing a strong community of believers. Please make it happen in my local church today. Amen.

Focus on Friendship

1. If you are an older woman, thoughtfully and prayerfully consider asking a younger woman if you can spend time together.
2. If you are a younger woman, thoughtfully and prayerfully consider asking an older woman to begin mentoring you.

3. If you are a younger woman, make a list of all the questions you would love to ask an older, wiser woman and then do so. If you are an older woman, recall your younger self and bring to mind the most pressing concerns you had as a young wife, mother, and/or working professional and pray for those areas in the younger woman's life you are now part of.

 *Chapter 12*

Peers Who Walk Alongside

One who has unreliable friends soon comes to ruin,
but there is a friend who sticks closer than a sister.
Proverbs 18:24

*Vulnerability brings with it an open door—one that
often remains closed in the normal busyness of our
lives. God intends for us to push open that door and step
boldly into a person's life when they need it most.*
Sarah Beckman

M e too!" Those are two mighty powerful words, which are made even more powerful when the person speaking them knows your deepest heartache and fearsome struggles. I'm so grateful for the women I call friends who have been with me in the midst of my lowest lows and highest highs. "Me too!" As you share your heart with a good friend, and even as you utter the last word, your friend is nodding her head in agreement and complete understanding, and she says, "Me too!" What a relief to simply know we are not alone in our struggle and pain.

I could recount story after story when one of my friends, my peers specifically, was dealing with exactly the same pressures and stresses in her life that I was experiencing in mine. When I was a young wife and mother, we were all trying to adjust ourselves, our mind-sets, and our lives—going from single to suddenly married. Many of my friends had children soon after they married, just as I did. Of course, this was another major life adjustment. That simple yet so life-impacting phrase "Me too!" was heard often between me and my closest friends.

Looking back on those early adulthood years, I can recognize how much I looked forward to Thursdays and Sundays when our church opened its doors for midweek activities and end of week worship and teaching. Thursday evenings, tired though I might be, were always worth the effort to load up my four kids to get them to their respective girls' and boys' groups so I could squeeze in a little mom-to-mom conversation with my friends before and after club meetings. Sundays, which seemed to always be hectic, were likewise another opportunity to catch up and swap stories with my friends.

I recall feeling so much better after talking with them about the ups and downs of daily life. I didn't have to waste time attempting to explain myself, my heartaches, or my fears. Why? Because my friends, my peers, were facing exactly the same scenarios in their own homes. One of the great blessings of having good friends who are also your peers is that you have good company to walk alongside you through every season of life. You never have to reach far to find a commiserating smile, a comforting hug, or a promise of prayer. With peers, it's just part of the package.

Of course, in order to take full advantage of your fellow peers' storehouse of experience and solutions and wise counsel, you have to be vulnerable yourself. I'm always amazed at how women function in a group setting. The rule of thumb seems to be that until one woman is brave enough to be honest about her pain and heartache, the rest of the group will remain on a guarded, rather shallow level. It only takes a single voice to share—sometimes through tears—what a deep hole she is in, before the entire group rallies around her in support. I've seen this phenomenon time after time.

One woman bravely sheds her superwoman cape and offers everyone in the room her gift of vulnerability and fragility. Then after she has been hugged and just plain loved on, the room quiets and another and another and another woman starts to open up. This is exactly how Jesus wants us to love and support one another! He wants each of us to find a few trusted friends who will speak his truth and life into our lives and keep on speaking until our final breaths.

There is no replacement in this life for developing peer-type friendships. Every single woman needs at least one, but hopefully many more—women who can and do with great regularity say to her heart and soul, "Me too!"

⟨♡⟩ *Take-away Action Thought*

I will be intentional about building and deepening friendships with my peers. I will also endeavor to live out my life with them in total transparency.

My Heart's Cry to You, O Lord

Father, I need to keep developing the friendships I have with those women who are going through challenges and struggles similar to mine. Help me to consistently ask each of them how they are doing and if I can help them. Remind me that whenever I feel like I'm the only one who is suffering, hurting, and confused that I am not. My peers and I are often in exactly the same situation in life, in marriage, in work, and in parenting. Remind me of how vulnerability can spark transparency in my friends so we can fully share and encourage one another. Show us what it means to have the type of community that Jesus desires for us. Amen.

Focus on Friendship

1. Work into your life consistent times to meet with your peers so you can have time and opportunity to share your hearts and your struggles and to pray for one another.

2. The next time you struggle with a personal issue, seek out your closest friends and share your heart with them. Allow your friends into your pain so you can talk together about life in general and today's issues specifically.

3. When you know that one of your peers is hurting and in a dark place, don't keep your distance hoping her problem will resolve itself. Instead, draw close to your friend and offer your heart, your listening ear, and your presence as a support to her.

Chapter 13

Younger, Teachable Friends to Mentor

Listen to advice and accept discipline,
and at the end you will be counted among the wise.
Proverbs 19:20

John was a voice for Christ with more than his voice.
His life matched his words. When a person's ways and
words are the same, the fusion is explosive. But when
a person says one thing and lives another, the result
is destructive. People will know we are Christians, not
because we bear the name, but because we live the life.

Max Lucado

About twenty years ago, I was in a weekly book discussion with a diverse group of women—younger, middle aged, and older. Since we were all reading and studying the same material, one would assume each of us would have similar responses to the reading. But we didn't. And here's why. The best aspect of this group probably wasn't even the books (though each one was terrific); it was the explosion of insight and synergy we all felt when we gathered together. The older women offered us younger to middle-aged participants something unique to their season of life: wisdom, experience, perspective, and maybe best of all, a learned peacefulness.

The younger women offered a contagious sense of energy and enthusiasm that we middle-aged to senior women "caught." Yes, these youthful women had the physical, emotional, and spiritual energy I fear some of us older women had left behind as we travailed through some hardships as yet not yet experienced by our younger counterparts. Together, regardless of the differences in our ages, all of us—young, middle aged, and older— reminded one another of many important spiritual truths and life lessons.

Remembering how uplifted I felt after meeting together, I still find it hard to understand why some women refuse to take part in gatherings with those of different age groups. What better way to navigate through many of life's most tangled and distressing life experiences than by rubbing shoulders and gleaning from those seasoned souls who have trekked the path ahead of you? Truly, there's nothing sweeter than immersing yourself in a gathering of Christ-following, God-honoring, prayer-warrior, biblically knowledgeable women. I should mention that we had loads of laughs along the way too. It wasn't just serious-minded, scholarly discussions (although we had those as well). As a group, we experienced the full gamut of life with and through one another.

I've been blessed and personally encouraged to have been (and am still being) mentored by a couple of older, godly women. I have a good number of peers who keep me plugging along, balance me out, speak truth into my life, pray for me, and remind me that every day can be a God-honoring, joy-full day because of Jesus. I've also taken on the role of mentor to some younger women over the years. Within these three types of female friendships, I consider myself immensely rich.

For those women of middle and senior age who aren't yet investing their life-store of wisdom and knowledge to a younger woman, I ask you to consider doing so. Perhaps you could try praying intentionally for God to bring you just the right young woman to befriend and offer your heart and hands to. Pray big and ask the Lord to orchestrate a meeting between you and a young woman who is in need of a guiding, loving older woman's care and perspective. You don't need to be rich, successful, or accomplished. What you do need is a passion for living your life in such a way that matches your words. You need to know the Lord Jesus personally and love him and his word passionately. You don't need to be able to impressively recite whole passages of Scripture. You just need to have a Bible that is getting worn through use and be able to search its pages for its life-giving principles. I heartily applaud any and all middle- to older-aged women who are already sharing their life lessons with younger women. I don't need to convince them how wonderful it is to spend time getting to know a younger woman and watch her blossom and grow strong in her faith over time. You already know you're getting the best part of the deal!

But for those of you who are scared to extend yourself to another, look back to a period in your own life when you would have given anything to have an older woman you could ask questions and receive advice. Be that mentor-type friend to someone today and watch what God will do in and through the friendship—in you and in your friend.

Take-away Action Thought

If I am not currently investing some time into the life of a younger woman, then I will begin praying for God to orchestrate a meeting between me and someone who needs encouraging.

My Heart's Cry to You, O Lord

Father, I have been personally blessed, loved, and encouraged by women of all different ages through the years. Older women have sweetly mentored me and in turn challenged me to find a friend younger than myself to mentor. Help me to never forget how much encouragement and strength it gave me to know that my older friends were praying me through some of my most painful seasons of life. Help me to remember how powerful it was to hear their stories and how they overcame hardships and suffering. It made my faith all the stronger! I want to be that type of inspiration and model of faith for younger women in my life. Show me who needs some support and help me to be there. Amen.

Focus on Friendship

1. If you were impacted by older women in your life, then you should seek out this kind of service to the younger women you meet. Keep your heart and eyes open to their struggles and their special needs.

2. Work to schedule in regular times to meet with younger women for coffee or lunch just because you care. Encourage them to use you as a sounding board for whatever they are facing in life.

3. If you're not in a relationship with a younger woman right now, then ask your friends, church family, or pastor if they know of a young woman who would be interested in meeting for Bible study or on an informal basis.

 *Chapter 14*

"In" Relationships: Those Who Disciple Us

My [daughter], do not despise the Lord's discipline,
and do not resent his rebuke,
because the Lord disciplines those he loves,
as a father the [daughter] he delights in.
Proverbs 3:11–12

*Many believe that suffering is never God's will. But
Scripture tells us that it often is. And these verses affirm
God's faithfulness even as we suffer. Unfortunately, most
of us don't give focused thought to evil and suffering
until we experience them. This forces us to formulate
perspective on the fly, at a time when our thinking is
muddled and we're exhausted and consumed by pressing
issues. If you've been there, you'll attest to the fact that
it's far better to think through suffering in advance.*

Randy Alcorn

Raise your hand if you relish the thought of pondering the unwelcome topic of suffering. The very last topic I want to dwell on is the inescapable fact of life that everyone suffers. We cannot get away from the global devastation that daily assaults victims and victimizers alike. Our morning newscasts start off with the grimmest details of crimes that occurred while we slept. Radio broadcasts blare warnings, unrest, and ongoing worldwide angst. Sometimes the suffering is just overwhelming.

So how does suffering in general relate to a book on women's friendships? Given the fact that all of us endure seasons of suffering, we should seek out the wisest among us to prepare our hearts and heads ahead of time. Each of needs to spend ample time studying God's word so we are fully equipped with the knowledge and understanding of who God is and continue to trust in him when he allows hardships to come into our lives.

The verse above says that God disciplines the sons and daughters he loves, just as parents discipline their children. We have the long view in mind when we raise our children and necessarily impose boundaries, rules, and discipline to protect them. We are most concerned about the development of their character, not simply for their survival but so they can thrive out in a world that rarely offers the kind of grace families can give. God, like parents, through the principles found in his word does the same. He offers us boundaries, rules, and discipline when we make choices that will harm us or others. He, like human parents, has the long view in mind, with an eternal perspective. Thus, hateful though it feels at times, we all endure suffering and possibly some discipline.

Given this truth, women need to have a few "in" friends in their inner circle. You know, the kind of friend you can call at 3:00 a.m. if you need to; the type of friend who will not only answer the phone at 3:00 a.m., but also won't hesitate to come to you in your darkest hour. These rare but wonderful "in" friends are truly that: "in" it for life. That's how they define friendship.

If you're not sure if you have an in-it-for-the-duration kind of friend, let me share a great life example. When I had my first shoulder surgery years earlier, I was so emotionally undone that I made almost daily phone calls to a good friend who had been through the same thing. She listened to me with patience, but then she would direct me right into biblical truth. She was kind, patient, gentle. She was also prepared to point me in the direction where I would find real healing—God's word. When I spoke despairingly, sometimes hopelessly, she would reframe my words using God's promises to supply all my needs. She literally spoke life back into my muddled and exhausted state. Thank the good Lord for my in-it-for-life friend.

You know if you have some in-it-for-life friends when you pick up right where you left off, even if it's been months since you last saw one another or communicated. Real friends of the "in" variety never have to waste time warming up their conversation by dull small talk about the weather. They jump right in where other (lesser) friends would never dare. Why? Because they are the kind of friend who loves us unconditionally. Any time. All the time. Even when we have little time together. Time is irrelevant. History, though, the shared history of "in" friends does matter. It's the invisible thread that binds two hearts together for the long haul. It's what we all need: friends who covenant with their hearts to be there "in" it today, tomorrow, and always.

Take-away Action Thought

I will spend some time reflecting on the quality of my friendships and ask myself if I am fulfilling the role of an "in" friend to my closest female friends?

My Heart's Cry to You, O Lord

Father, help me to be diligent in studying the Scriptures so that I know who you are and try to grasp why suffering will always be a part of our broken world. Help me to not run away from this truth, but as much as I am able help me to equip myself by wisely meditating and memorizing your word so that I can speak out biblical truth when I am suffering. Help me to be the kind of "in" friend I must be to those closest to me. Help me to never shirk a difficult conversation with a friend I love who is struggling or straying from you. Give me the gentleness, kindness, and compassion I need to communicate your constant love and care to anyone who questions that. Keep me on target every day, and don't let me grow weary of investing myself in the friendships you've blessed me with. Amen.

Focus on Friendship

1. As you sit before the Lord, spend time asking him to reveal to you if you are fulfilling the godly role of an "in-it-for-life" kind of friend to the women you hold dearest in this life. If you aren't, then make the needed changes to give these precious friendships a higher priority in your life.

2. By definition, an "in" friend is willing (uncomfortable as it may be) to gently offer biblical direction and correction to a friend who is not making godly choices. Because you truly love your friend and want what is best for her, pray for the courage to be open and upfront about any issues you are concerned about.

3. Make it your mission to be a teachable, humble friend who accepts the corrective direction and exhortation from an "in" friend. Pray for the grace to not become defensive or angry if/when a friend feels compelled to offer her counsel to you.

 # Chapter 15

"Out" Relationships: Those We Evangelize and Invite to Christ

Gracious words are a honeycomb,
sweet to the soul and healing to the bones.

Proverbs 16:24

Be faithful to watch for times when God is asking you to shine His light to a hurting soul, and you'll find opportunities everywhere. Let's walk humbly and act bravely in the face of another's need, whether we know the state of their faith or not.

Sarah Beckman

I n the last chapter, we discussed what "in" relationships look like, how fellow Christ believers come close to us and take on the necessary roles of supporting, loving, encouraging, and, when needed, redirecting, rebuking, and even on some occasions admonishing us to take another look at our attitude and actions in the bright light of God's word and of eternity. For sure, our "in" relationships are essential ones.

Now let's consider the value (to others as well as ourselves) of making, cultivating, and investing in "out" friendships. What exactly is an "out" type of friendship? Simply put, a friend who doesn't share one's faith in Jesus Christ. She could be your favorite neighbor, your closest cousin, your work colleague, or your talented hair stylist. It doesn't make a whit of difference where or how you met your friend. What does matter is that you ask the Lord to keep you sensitive to opportunities to open the door to conversing about what your faith in Christ means to you personally.

I remember when I was a much younger woman working full time at a large company in an accounting department with fifteen other women from every ethnic, education, social, and economic background. We were a diverse group indeed. I learned so much about people in general during those three and a half years. I was one of the "young gals" and there were three of us. The rest of the group had been longtime employees, and many had been in this same department for over twenty-plus years. Some of us were there to gain some experience before moving on, while others were at the stopping point of their careers and eagerly awaiting retirement. There was a night and day difference between us.

At that point in my life, I had more emotional zeal than I had life experience, and I wince at how I spoke with great passion about the faithfulness of God, which probably came across as a youthful naivety. One woman I became friends with had recently been abandoned by her husband of many years, leaving her with two teenagers, lots of debt, and jobless. She was a temporary staff employee in the department where I worked, so I shared my heart with her and what was most important to my heart: Jesus. Looking back, I'm confident that my youth, my delivery, and my lack of life experience turned her off completely. In fact, when she told me to change the subject, I got the picture she didn't want to hear about Jesus.

Recalling my then-inexperienced younger self, I realize I should have spent more time and effort just loving and listening to her and becoming her friend. But I was impatient and wanted her to know Jesus because I thought he would solve all her problems and give her rebirth from the inside out. I now wish I had taken a gentler, quieter, side-door approach to introducing her to my Savior. While I can't go back in time, I can certainly learn from my mistakes.

If you're like me, you may have some epic failures in your own sharing-your-faith résumé with someone you care deeply about. If you're also like me, you may feel gun-shy after being rejected, especially when you just cared so much that you wanted your friend to know the Savior too. There's nothing to be ashamed of in that, but maybe we could all work a little harder in our delivery. If we take the time to reflect on the ways and means in which others have approached us with something they're passionate about, we may learn from our own reaction to them. I'm all for listening to someone share her heart, her concerns, and her passions with me, but honestly I am a lot more receptive when the delivery is right.

What exactly makes for a good delivery of an important message? It all begins with bathing the conversation in prayer ahead of time—for your sake and for your listener's sake. Ask God to help you be great in wisdom and few in words. Ask him to help you place yourself in your friend's position in order to see life from their perspective or pain. Then ask for a humble, meek, gentle, compassionate heart and mind before you utter a single word. Let your very presence radiate Jesus' love to your friend. In whatever ways God has opened doors of opportunity for you to serve your friend by meeting practical needs in their lives, make sure you've invested yourself there too. Let your words and deeds match up to the message you want to share.

In short, be the kind of friend you want in others. Faithful and true. A confidence keeper. Never a gossip. Not a complainer or a grumbler. Be thankful, humble, gentle, and kind. Let your life shine because Jesus lives in your heart. It should be his love that radiates winsomely, happily, and generously from you.

 Take-away Action Thought

I will ask the Lord to make me sensitive to opportunities to serve my friends who do not yet know Jesus.

My Heart's Cry to You, O Lord

Father, I am sometimes afraid to share my faith with those women in my life who have suffered far more than I have. I am scared they will look at me and assume I haven't been through the pain they have endured. Help me to keep my heart in tune with the Holy Spirit's gentle nudges to share in ways that will draw my friends to Jesus. Give me opportunities to serve these women in practical ways, and give me the strength to consistently give without expecting anything in return. Lord, my heart's desire is for every woman with whom I rub shoulders to know you, love you, and serve you. For them and their eternal security in Christ I pray. Amen.

Focus on Friendship

1. Ask the Lord to keep you alert and always ready to step in and meet the practical needs your friends may have, if you are able to do so.

2. Purpose to pray daily for each of your unbelieving friends and live with an expectancy that God is working in their hearts and minds to draw them to him.

3. Ask God to prepare your heart, mind, and words to gently and compassionately share your faith with your friends as the Holy Spirit leads you.

 *Chapter 16*

Different Friends for Different Seasons

Let the wise listen and add to their learning,
and let the discerning get guidance.

Proverbs 1:5

*Folks in trial don't necessarily want fixing, especially
in "unfixable" situations like illness or death. When you
jump to "I can help you make this better," it frustrates
them. They feel you're trivializing their troubles. There
is a time and a place for advice/suggestions, but if
you want to stand out from a crowd and love your
neighbor well in their trial, start by listening.*

Sarah Beckman

I had a good friend who came into my life for what I call a short season. We were introduced and became "fast friends." We were seemingly on the same page with every issue that mattered most in life. I wasn't able to see her often, but whenever we got the chance to meet up we talked until someone had to literally pull us apart. Enjoying our friendship, we looked ahead through the years to when we would be married with children, still calling each other for advice or simply to talk—and talk and talk!

79

But our forever friendship wasn't to be. No, we didn't have a disagreement or an argument that severed the relationship. Due to a life-changing and heartbreaking set of circumstances, my friend decided to move to another state to heal. This broke her heart and it broke mine as well. In a matter of a few weeks, she had packed up and left me behind. I was sad, disheartened, depressed, and grieving. On so many fronts, this situation just hurt.

Who would ever have guessed that God would allow the scenario to play out as it did? Not me. Here I was thinking that I was adding another traveling companion for life to my deep-end friendship pool. But this wasn't to be. The hardest aspect of my friend's departure was that while I had no part in her decision to leave town, I was a reminder of her pain. So she needed to distance herself from me too! Not only did I no longer have a friendship I treasured, but I also had to give her the time and space to heal apart from me.

I cried many tears over the seeming injustice of this whole situation. I ranted at God in my not-so-fine moments. I pleaded with Jesus to make it all right again. I begged the Lord to heal my friend's heart completely—and do it yesterday, please. Yes, I went through the gamut of wild emotions before I finally accepted the situation and made peace with it (and God). But it took a toll on me. I learned much, however, in the months and years that followed. I slowly began to accept the fact that life is always in motion and I should live in humble gratitude for today (and for today's friendships, family, and other blessings God has bestowed). On every level, we have only this day.

Different friends for different seasons. Sometimes folks enter our lives for the duration and others dip in and out, while still others are briefly in our circle of friends, never to return. I believe the importance of this life truth is to learn to discipline our expectations by honing grateful hearts. God in his word never guarantees us forever friendships. What he does offer us is the promise that he will never leave us. That's a big difference.

Our problem arises when we muddy the waters with our "it's my right" type of expectation as it pertains to friends. Given the situation I described above, I have come to recognize that my small bit role in my good friend's moment of crisis was perhaps to have been a good friend with a listening ear. Because we were friends, she poured out her heart to me. Since we had already been sharing confidences all along, it was natural for her to be honest with me in this difficult situation. I knew I couldn't ease her pain, and I was well aware I couldn't change the situation. But I knew I could sit quietly, hold her hand, and listen well. Listen long. Listen intently.

For all of us who have friends who have been a part of our lives only for a season or two, let me challenge you to thank the Lord for the time you had with your friend. Ask him to give you his eternal perspective to help you walk through any heartaches or painful partings. If the situation allows, try to keep in touch with your friend long-distance. Although the friendship has changed in space and form, in many cases it need not end. Step up to the challenge and face the fact that life is always in motion; walk forward into the future, confident that the former strengths you found in friendships will sustain you in your tomorrows.

Take-away Action Thought

I will not stay in a place of ongoing grief if one of my friendships ends. Instead, I will purpose to be grateful for the precious time we shared.

My Heart's Cry to You, O Lord

Father, help me to process this hard transition in my life. I honestly miss the presence of a good friend and feel her loss keenly. It just plain hurts, and I feel shocked that this friendship is seemingly over. It hurts all the more because we didn't disagree or argue; our separation was due to a situation beyond our control. Perhaps we can remake our friendship to accommodate the changes that have occurred—or maybe not. Lord, help me to accept this change with good grace. Help me to listen well to my friend's heart and not try to fix the situation but leave it in your capable hands. Help us both to trust you with this change and be intentional about developing grateful hearts for the time we did share as friends. Amen.

Focus on Friendship

1. Be intentional about being a good listener and stop yourself if you are tempted to short-circuit the conversation to try and fix your friend's pain and suffering.
2. Purpose to accept that life is always changing, which includes your friends and the decisions they have to make at important junctures of their lives.
3. Ask the Lord what he wants to teach you through this parting, and seek to honor him by trusting in what he allows into your life.

 *Chapter 17*

Different Friends for Different Purposes

Know also that wisdom is like honey for you:
If you find it, there is a future hope for you,
and your hope will not be cut off.

Proverbs 24:14

*We won't be in any relationship long before our selfishness
starts to show—or real sacrifice is called for. If we
ever grow up, we will have to grow up together.*

Paula Rinehart

*H*ave you ever felt the need to talk to a good friend? You just wanted someone to listen without judgment, nod her head in agreement at the appropriate moments, reaffirm her loyalty to you, and tell you that your perspective was the accurate one. I've had lots of those "I-just-need-to-talk-with-my-friend today" moments in life. For the most part, I haven't been disappointed when I shared my heart with a good friend. But then there have been times it didn't quite work out as I had hoped.

I recall one singular conversation with a wonderful friend when I had all of the expectations cited above as I started sharing my heart of hearts with her. It was quickly dashed to pieces when my friend began to ask me insightful, directed questions about the problem I was facing (and the frustrations I was experiencing). All of a sudden, I felt as if I was sitting underneath an interrogation lamp and my friend was shining the spotlight not on my problem (and those who were causing it) but on me. It seemed as though the problem faded entirely into the background and my (poor) attitude and suggested plan of action (also poor) to remedy said problem were now the main thrust of the conversation.

I sat there in disbelief, wondering what was going on in my mind and in my friend's mind. What just happened? Did I miss something? More accurately, did I say something amiss? As I sat there trying to process my turbulent surge of emotions, I realized that my friend was trying her best to get me to see past the current troubling situation and into the deeper root causes of my heart's unrest. Probably because I was still in a tiny bit of shock at how this conversation was playing out, I sat there trying my best to listen to my friend's heart behind her words.

After a while, I recognized the power of assumption and of expectation. I had been full of them both. Never did I even consider that my friend might feel compelled to aim the shining light of biblical truth in my direction. I assumed she would side with me, help soothe my emotional wounds, and take my side. Evidently, I have more skill in choosing faithful friends than I give myself credit for, because while my expectations were dashed during this conversation something better emerged: trust, loyalty, and faithfulness. My friend was showing her true colors by displaying the power and beauty of God's word as it applied to my situation and my heart condition. In the space of that single chat with my friend, I realized how much she cared about me in the long view of life (and life eternal). She wasn't willing to stand by and let me make a mess of an already difficult situation, so she went courageously right to the heart of the matter.

God brings us different friends for different purposes in our lives. Have you thanked him for that? My friend who loved me enough to challenge my thoughts and my proposed actions was God's agent of rescue to my struggling, pained heart. I'm very grateful to him for it! Other times, I've had friends come to me during seasons when I was at an impasse in my marriage and didn't know how my husband and I would resolve a high-priority issue. Along came my older friend who seemed to see directly into my heart without me having to say a word; she first loved on me and then began peppering me with questions that told me she knew of what she spoke (and asked). And I walked away feeling energized and determined to work through this problem with my husband. Thank God!

Another friend recognized how discouraged I was with a ministry I was leading, and she offered her own kind counsel by sharing with me how she dealt with a similar problem over the past year. Again, this friend who had experienced my same struggle helped me to work through it and grow stronger because of it. Thank God! Still another friend had the courage to inquire about how much time I'd been spending with the Lord away from work and family responsibilities, because she had noted my increasing irritability and critical-minded spirit. Again, thank God!

All of the above friends in each and every one of the circumstances was working as God's agent of rescue in my life. Different friends for different purposes. Let's rejoice that God is always working to meet our every need, and that he uses our best friends to recognize our neediness and offer gentleness, kindness, hope, and lots of unconditional love. It's true what Paula Rinehart says above. If you and I are going to grow up (in character and in our faith), then we will have to grow up together.

 ## Take-away Action Thought

I will purpose to be accepting and graciously hear the words of exhortation and rebuke when my good friends notice something amiss in my heart's attitude.

My Heart's Cry to You, O Lord

Father, help me to be ready to accept wise counsel and advice from my friends who only want what is best for me. Make my heart tender and sensitive to the wisdom that my good friends offer me because they love me with a faithful biblical love. I know that it is hard for them to approach me with a sensitive issue they believe is harming me. I also don't want to become hardened toward my friends who are honoring the principles found in your word about faithfully loving one's friends. Give me a heart that is teachable at all times, especially when I feel hurt or am struggling to work through a difficult situation. I know that my friends have been sent by you to be your hands and feet, sent to rescue me from myself and my blindness concerning my own areas of sinfulness. Amen.

Focus on Friendship

1. Pray for a spirit of humility, meekness, and teachability so that you are truly open to hearing good counsel

from your friends when they approach you with their observations or concerns.

2. Desire to be the type of friend who thanks God for sending friends to you as his agents of rescue by being keenly aware that he is nudging them to speak to you on his behalf.

3. Don't harbor unrealistic expectations or make assumptions about how conversations will play out when you speak with your friends about the challenges you are facing.

 # Chapter 18

Make-Me-Laugh, Let's-Have-Fun Friends

Light in a messenger's eyes brings joy to the heart,
and good news gives health to the bones.

Proverbs 15:30

*Courage is the face of love when it invites the other person
into growth and freedom—which, for a Christian, means
that you are learning to actively trust God in the place
where old fears and insecurities have controlled you.*

Paula Rinehart

I have a friend who knows how to make me laugh. I mean laugh until my-sides-hurt-kind of laugh. The type of laugh that makes you feel better inside about, well, everything. It's the same kind of laugh small children engage in throughout the day and that most adults stop doing when they reach adulthood. The kind of comic feeling that, when you experience it, you wish there were more reasons to laugh full and free each and every day.

There is and are more reasons to laugh full and free every day. Each of us needs a friend (or two) who have the unique ability to make us, others, and themselves laugh hard and long.

It may be the kind of quirky way they view life and how they look at problems in particular. Or it may be that God just designed these funny folks with a higher caliber of making life merry. What I do understand and appreciate is this: the friends who can make me laugh lighten my load considerably, and I leave them feeling better about my life and wanting to pass on the same contagious sense of joy they sparked in me.

Back to my friend I mentioned at the beginning of this chapter. I'd love for you to meet her. She has the sunniest disposition, and her face seems lit up with happiness from deep within. People don't even need to hear her speak; her very presence is uplifting and encouraging. That's not to say she hasn't endured her share of difficult times and long seasons of suffering. But my friend hasn't allowed these hard times to dim that inner light of Jesus' love for life in general and people in particular. Remember that old children's song, "This Little Light of Mine"? That describes my friend perfectly. She knows how to let it shine, let it shine, let it shine!

I hope you have a friend (or two) who makes you laugh when all you want to do is cry. I hope that God has blessed you with a friend (or two) who has a sunny disposition so contagious that you are uplifted by just being in her presence. Maybe you are that friend to others. Perhaps God has blessed you with an innate ability to see life from a sunny-side up perspective, and there is nothing you enjoy more than helping others view life from the same vantage point.

But for those who don't have friends who can make them laugh, don't be dismayed. There are ways to find reasons for smiling, for laughing, for finding humor everywhere you look.

No, I'm not talking about laughing at others' quirky habits or honing a witty sarcastic comeback. Making fun of others is never right. Rather, I'm talking about how to lighten up and laugh at ourselves more often. Instead of automatically feeling frustrated or embarrassed when we make a mistake or fumble at something, why not learn to smile away the situation and thank the Lord it wasn't worse? How about laughing more often at the often ironic turns of life? When we get caught in traffic, instead of allowing our anxiety levels to rule the moment, why not prepare for such events by having some (clean) comedy CDs ready to pop in while you wait? Why not? Are we afraid to let loose and experience the freedom of laughter? Do we somehow believe that Christians don't laugh? After all, Jesus laughed and he is God!

Laughter is not only good for our soul, but it also has excellent health benefits. If you don't believe me, search the Internet for the bonuses of laughing more every day and you'll be surprised. Rather than confining your conversation to the serious-only topics of the day, become an expert at spotting the hilarious among the mundane. Do it for yourself. Do it for your family. Do it for your friends. Learn and relearn to love laughter.

Take-away Action Thought

I will look for the comedic in everyday happenings and will pass along the funny stories to my family and my friends.

My Heart's Cry to You, O Lord

Father, you know how much my mood lightens after a good long laugh. It doesn't seem to matter whether I am laughing at something silly I did or in response to a friend's funny take on life. It just feels so good to belly laugh. I need to be the kind of friend my friends can laugh with together. Lord, help me to see the funny side to more and more of life's situations, and help me to discipline myself to be positive and optimistic about whatever may frustrate me. I pray that each of us would see the health benefits of laughter and put more effort into looking for laughter as a way to feel better inside and out. Show us how to appreciate the power of a good laugh and make it a daily habit. Amen.

Focus on Friendship

1. Spend some time looking for funny stories, jokes, and movies, and then consistently make reading, listening, and viewing whatever makes you laugh a regular part of your life.
2. Be the kind of friend who can feel at ease laughing at yourself and will stop taking yourself so seriously.
3. If your friends need to laugh, be creative in finding out what makes them giggle and encourage them to see life from a funnier perspective.

Chapter 19

Inspire-Me, Challenge-Me Friends

Trust in the Lord with all your heart
and lean not on your own understanding;
in all your ways acknowledge him,
and he will make your paths straight.

Proverbs 3:5–6

The river of the Spirit of God overcomes all obstacles.
Never focus your eyes on the obstacle or the difficulty. The
obstacle will be a matter of total indifference to the river
that will flow steadily through you if you will simply
remember to stay focused on the Source. If you believe in
Jesus, you will find that God has developed and nourished
in you mighty, rushing rivers of blessing for others.

Oswald Chambers

Sometimes, we may wonder if a person God has placed in our life is really a friend—not because she lacks in the caring department, but because her delivery is way off. Lord, help us when this kind of friend spots a weakness in our character or a minor lapse in our judgment! She will let us know exactly what she thinks about the situation. In fact, this kind of friend, well-meaning and all, is often the only one brave enough to speak out when we may be faltering in a decision or when our attitude misses the mark of godly living.

I had a friend like this once, and to be honest there were moments in our friendship when I did wonder if I might be better off without her rather blunt comments and harsh suggestions. And yet, God used this woman to push me to greater depths of introspection when I needed it most. I remember being at the crossroads of having to make a decision that would impact me and my family. It was increasingly wearing on me as the deadline drew closer. My friend recognized my internal angst, my ever-escalating level of worry, and how preoccupied I had become. She told me so in short order.

I have to admit that my first desire was to school her in softening her manner, but I didn't. I took my medicine, so to speak. Then I took her words (which I was confident she spoke because she truly cared about me) to heart as well. I prayed, I worked through Scripture, and I had an attitude adjustment that was long overdue. While my friend stopped short of offering me advice on what decision to make, she did help me to see the larger frame of the situation.

My friend challenged me to put my focus on the Lord, his never-changing character, and his absolute promise to be with me and provide for me no matter what I decided. My friend, who knew my sinful tendency to try and control anything and everything (thus diminishing risk to myself), pretty much scolded me and then reminded me of God's sovereignty. It was exactly what I needed to hear. My friend, who has come a long way in her delivery process over the years, has hopefully seen growth in me as well. I'm sure, however, that if I ever begin to falter and misstep by placing myself in the control seat of my life, she will faithfully remind me that only God sits in that chair.

Friends can be tricky life commodities. We all need a few friends who will rise to the challenge if we need a gentle nudge in a new direction. Feeling stuck? Discouraged? Defeated? Feel like giving up? Depressed? Downhearted? Enter in that stalwart inspire-me, challenge-me, type of gal pal. Most women have at least a few of these bold-as-brass but loyal-to-a-fault friends. You know the type. Those people who never lack in the courage department when they spot a friend on the verge of making a terrible mistake in judgment. This friend lays it out on the table.

The challenge usually isn't whether or not her advice is worth heeding. Rather, the challenge is if we can handle how she delivers her message with an often-brusque manner. I'd like to believe that I've never been on the poor delivery side of the equation with my friends. But I can tell you to my own personal disappointment that I've failed in delivering information, instruction, admonition, and suggestions to my friends and family. How do I know this? They've told me so. Which brings up an entirely added layer to the discussion on friendships: how we treat our family (our in-home private friendship core group) matters.

I've been challenged by my loved ones as well when I grouse over hurt feelings or shock at a blunt rebuke from one of my inspire-me, challenge-me friends, and I turn around and speak just as bluntly to them. The bottom line is that God faithfully surrounds us with voices of truth, and it's up to us to develop a thick enough skin to handle their well-meaning words with grace (because we know that they care). So the next time one of your inspire-me, challenge-me friends speaks out with bold conviction, try not to react. Instead, respond by thanking her for loving you so well—and mean it.

Take-away Action Thought

I will purpose to develop a thicker skin as it pertains to the direct words of admonishment and challenges from those friends I know love me enough to tackle these sensitive issues.

My Heart's Cry to You, O Lord

Father, help me to be discerning enough to identify those friends who love me enough to speak directly to me because they deeply care about me. If I have some women in my life who don't truly want the best for me but speak words that wound or harm me, give me the good sense to distance myself from them. Help me to hone thick enough skin so I'm not undone by the kindness of truthful observations that direct me to you and your word. I am grateful for those friends who love me so much that they speak up when they observe something amiss in my heart's attitude, my words, or my actions. Help us all to use our words as life-giving instruments of change, give us great self-control, and let these alterations begin at home. Amen.

Focus on Friendship

1. Purpose to be a discerning friend and not take offence when a friend of comes to you with concerns about your attitudes, words, and actions.
2. Desire to be the kind of friend courageous enough to gently confront a friend when you see her moving into dangerous territory.
3. Model self-control and self-restraint in how you use your words.

 ## Chapter 20

Give-Me-Roots, Give-Me-Wings Friends

My [daughter], do not let wisdom
and understanding out of your sight,
preserve sound judgment and discretion;
they will be life for you,
an ornament to grace your neck.
Then you will go on your way in safety,
and your foot will not stumble.
When you lie down, you will not be afraid;
when you lie down, your sleep will be sweet.
Proverbs 3:21–24

*I am not, nor do I have to be, Superwoman. I have
limits, and I'd do well to adhere to them.*
Sarah Beckman

My hope and prayer for every woman who picks up
this book has at least one friend who has shared
history with her and so gives her roots. And because of how well she knows the other's heart, she gives her
wings. Roots are necessary, because where we came from matters. Our family of origin is important, and we need to recognize

those daily patterns of life where we learned how to resolve conflict, work through disappointment, stay committed (even when it would be easier to walk away), and forgive when hurt by someone who says they love you. Every one of these patterns for working through whatever problem you have will in part determine who you choose for a mate, how you decide to parent your children, what kind of vocation to follow, and how you govern your life in a million different ways. Roots matter, and having a friend from way back when is perhaps one of God's finest gifts to us women.

Another essential aspect in each woman's friend arsenal is to have a friend who gives us wings—one who hones in on our sometimes subtly hidden talents, gifts, and abilities, and who helps us develop those for the enrichment of others' lives (and our own). Your own particular give-me-wings friend will also be on the lookout every time your gifts shine through work, family, and ministry. She will happily lift you up so you feel it's possible to step out in faith when the next opportunity arises. Or perhaps your friend will mentor you personally so you are fully equipped to take over when she decides to step aside.

Yes indeed, every woman needs a friend (or two or more) who provides a solid foundation of shared history to help you both work through any past childhood or growing-up issues that continue to hinder you from living the full life God intends. We also need a friend (or two or more) who provides the positivity and insight that gives us the strength to go after God-inspired goals and dreams. If you have these two friends, the sky literally is the limit.

I have a friend (or two or more) who continues to provide both roots and wings in my life. I am blessed. Often, I can envision a new concept or an idea I believe would strengthen and enrich other Christ followers' lives. Then, after that initial burst of creative energy, I sometimes begin doubting my ability to pull it off. During these moments of feeling unsure and incapable of seeing my projected ideas through to completion, my friends walk me through my own timeline of history and help me to remember that I felt the same way fifteen years, ten years, five years, even a year ago. Then they begin sparking my memory by describing how I overcame other obstacles and how God met my every need all through the process. I am indeed blessed.

This friend will also help me identify the specific gifts and talents God has placed within me. She will share specific incidents when I used my talents in ministry and God blessed the outcome. Or, more meaningful still, she will emotionally recall times when I served her using whatever God had given me as a source of help and encouragement in her time of need. Consider making more intentional effort to become the type of friend who offers both roots and wings to a few of your closest friends. They will call themselves blessed.

 Take-away Action Thought

I will heed my wise friends who share a history with me that gives me roots and who help me to look ahead with confidence and hope in what may be in the future.

My Heart's Cry to You, O Lord

Father, I need your help in working through any past disappointments, childhood trauma, or pain in my life so I can live fully and live free. Help me to rightly and accurately examine the life patterns I fall back on that may be unwise or even harmful to me and those I love. Give me ears to hear when my closest friends ask me to listen to what they have to say about my past and how it could affect my future. I pray also for the courage to step into the unknown future if you ask me to, Lord. I want to use every gift, talent, and resource you have given me to build your kingdom. Help me to be mindful of my dear friends' encouraging words, offering them the same exhortation and confidence they have given me. Amen.

Focus on Friendship

1. Take heed to whatever your closest friends share with you about their observations about how your childhood and family of origin may still affect you today.
2. Be thankful for those sincere friends who take the time to offer you words of exhortation and encouragement. Bless them in like manner.
3. Today, pray for your roots-and-wings friends, asking that the Lord will richly provide friends for them to meet their needs in the same way they have met yours.

Part Three

How to Become a Friend Who Stays the Distance

 *Chapter 21*

Pray for the Right Friends
(Then Pray for Your Friends)

Perfume and incense bring joy to the heart,
and the pleasantness of a friend
springs from their heartfelt advice.

Proverbs 27:9

*God asks us to walk with him through the blood and guts
of our real experience in an honest pilgrimage where we let
him show us what real strength, and real love, are all about.*

Paula Rinehart

One of the primary motivations for me to write this book is to talk about the enduring friendships in my life, and how happy and blessed they have made me. However, as I participate in women's groups, lead small group studies, interview women for my work, and just rub shoulders with females through everyday life happenings, I'm also keenly aware that some women have no real friends in their lives—which makes me want to cry.

Life is hard enough with the company of a select group of faithful friends at your side. I can't imagine enduring my trials and seasons of suffering without my friends at my side, both figuratively and literally. Friends—real friends—can make or break a woman. For this purpose, I believe it is essential for all women to be mindful about including their friends as part of their regular prayer lives.

How do we do this? To begin, if you don't have a journal, buy one. Then open it up and list each of your friends, leaving a page for each person. Write down any current struggles or specific needs they have today, and then date these prayers/requests. Then as a part of your daily prayer time, spend a few minutes "praying through" your friends' pages, asking God to strengthen, give grace, offer insight and wisdom, provide a job, restore a marriage, or bring a wayward child back home. Whatever "it" is that your friends are in need of, become a prayer warrior on their behalf.

When we are at our lowest, we can find it difficult to pray articulately or specifically because we're so lost in our own pain. This is the perfect time for friends to step up and become the intercessors to the throne of grace for us. Step up when your friends are unable to do so. Pray "up" on behalf of your friends. The friend you pray for today will then be the faith-graced woman who prays for you tomorrow.

If you are a woman struggling to connect with other women in a meaningful way, may I suggest you take your painful situation to the Lord in prayer? We know from what we learn in the Scriptures that God wants us to live in community with one another. There are no exceptions to this rule of life. Perhaps you are a woman who has always enjoyed rich female friendships, but you recently moved to a new city and it has been a difficult transition, so making friends hasn't been at the top of your list. Or you may now be in your senior years, and the majority of your friends have passed away. Possibly you are in the midst of a long-term caregiving season with no visible end in sight, and you don't have the energy to restart old friendships or find new ones. May I once again challenge you to rethink any resistance or even legitimate reasons for not actively finding ways to connect with other women?

Whatever obstacles you are facing in your life situation, you (and I) are far better equipped to handle these challenges with good grace when we have friends we can call, text, e-mail, or visit for a quick pep talk or word of encouragement. Life just flows more smoothly when good friends—praying friends to be precise—are part of the mix. If you really have no energy to take up a hobby, then join a women's group or work out at a local gym where you might meet other women. Pray for the Lord to bring Christ-following women across your path. Ask God to orchestrate meetings between you and a few other women in his way and in his time. Never stop praying for believing friends to become part of this season of your life. Pray with expectancy. Pray with boldness. Pray with confidence. Pray because God's word tells us to pray without ceasing.

Take-away Action Thought

Whatever season of life I am in, I will pray intently for God to bring female friends into my life so we can encourage one another in this journey.

My Heart's Cry to You, O Lord

Father, I'm in the midst of so many changes that many of my friends are no longer part of my life. It's not that I've neglected my friendships, but I have been burdened with a heavy load of caregiving and working and moving. I haven't had time to invest in trying to meet new women to take the place of those friends I've lost. Help me to find simple ways to intersect with other like-minded Christ followers, and help me to be open to new doors of friendship when you open them. I pray I will recognize opportunities to explore new hobbies, volunteering, and church-related ministries where I might more naturally get acquainted with women with whom I may share a lot in common. I pray, expecting you hear my prayer and will answer my heart's cry for friendship. Amen.

Focus on Friendship

1. Don't stop looking for practical ways to meet new women that may have much in common with you; be open to developing new friendships along the way.
2. Right now, pray for the friends in your life today; don't neglect to bring them and their needs before the throne of grace daily.
3. Focus on being content wherever God has placed you in this life, secure that he will supply your every need.

 # Chapter 22

Love Unconditionally
(Accept Each Other's Differences with Grace)

Love covers all wrongs.
Proverbs 10:12b

While I disparage the exercise of "building one's
self-esteem" I indulge in it every time I imagine myself
free from the defects I perceive in someone else. I am, in
effect, thanking God that I am not like him or her.
Elisabeth Elliot

I had a friend whose friendship I treasured during a time when we were both still in college, unmarried, and trying to figure out life's next steps. We traversed that uncertain youthful season together, encouraging each other along the way. Both of us were growing in our faith, trying to figure out where and how God wanted to use our respective gifts and talents. For the most part, my friend and I agreed on the big factors of life. We were (and still are) like-minded Christ followers.

After some years passed, we both married and had children, set up our homes and, once again (because it was another new season of life), tried to figure out what marriage and parenting as Christian women looked like. It was at this point in our lives when we began to diverge in the choices we made for our respective families. My friend was opposed to some of my preferences and, honestly, I viewed some of hers as nonissues in the greater scheme of life.

You can probably guess what happened over time. Our once intimate friendship waned into a more casual acquaintance. Although neither of us "ended" the friendship, nor did we take issue with each other's choices, eventually our specific preferences for our individual families drifted us apart. Over the years, I've pondered how we might have changed the outcome of our relationship, but I realize today that we both grew up and changed as people. There wasn't anything sinful or wrong in either of our choices—they were simply different. To be truthful, I'm just fine with that.

Some almost thirty years later, I can truthfully say that my friend and I are genuinely happy to see each other (when we run into each other) and we can seemingly pick right up where we left off. We both realize that we have grown and changed as individuals, but we understand we can still honor and respect each other's choices. Today, my friend and I are absolutely fine with how our friendship has (or hasn't) played out over time.

When I look back, however, I see that there were moments during our "transitional friendship phase" when I sometimes felt misunderstood. I knew my friend's heart was always in the right place, even when we disagreed on the particulars of marriage and child rearing. That underlying confidence in her consistent love for the Lord and for me as her friend was indeed a healing balm whenever I lamented our languishing friendship.

I believe God was working actively in both of our hearts to help us to regard each other with respect, giving grace even when we disagreed. He knew how easily it would be for us to slip into the role that delights the enemy—that of judge and jury rolled into one. It could have happened so subtly that neither my friend nor I may have even been aware of the attitude shift in our hearts toward the other. But God graciously tugged at my heartstrings when I was tempted to hold a private pity party for myself, crying ugly tears about feeling misunderstood. Instead, the Holy Spirit spoke to my heart with gentle reminders that my friend might be feeling the same way. Was she feeling hurt by the growing chasm between us because of the choices we were making for our families?

I am sure she was, because we talked about it on occasion. What a relief to actually say the words out loud to each other. Once we were honest enough to share our hearts, I believe we both made peace with how our friendship was morphing. I remember with relief and gratitude how God gave us the grace to converse gently, kindly, and with respect. There will always be differences in our lives, but never animosity—thanks to the mercies of God.

 *Take-away Action Thought*

I will find ways to build bridges with a friend, even when we don't agree on lifestyle preferences. I will not allow myself to build a wall between us.

My Heart's Cry to You, O Lord

Father, you know the situation between my friend and me. We are both growing and changing so much that there are moments when I wonder at the state of our friendship. Can it survive? Can we find a way to maintain this relationship when we have begun to take such diverging paths in life? Although neither of us is walking away from you or your biblical principles, we are actively making different types of choices for our respective families—and it stings a little. Help us both to offer the other ongoing respect and understanding, even when we don't understand. Show us how to love each other although we might be in total disagreement about how we choose to live out our faith. Amen.

Focus on Friendship

1. Pray to be purposeful about not falling into the trap of judging your friend when she chooses to make decisions you disagree with. Instead, offer her all the encouragement you can when it is appropriate to do so.

2. Love your friend, despite how you are both changing and growing apart. Even though you may choose to live out your faith in different ways, never speak of her in a negative manner.

3. Consistently pray for your friend, her family, and your friendship—that even though it is changing in form, it will continue to be a Christ-honoring relationship.

 *Chapter 23*

Forgive Generously
(Forgive Because You Have Been Forgiven)

A heart at peace gives life to the body.
Proverbs 14:30a

*Has the clock stopped in your life? Was there a moment
when someone or something hurt you—and everything
changed? Perhaps you can still remember the day, the
time, the year, the scenery, the circumstances. Your hopes,
dreams, and innocence felt the sharp sting of betrayal and
disappointment. Ever since, the story of your life has been
to recapture your loss and seek your revenge, either through
outright action or the withholding of love and affection.*
Nancy Leigh DeMoss

Been there, done that. I'm sorry to say that I still re-
peatedly nurse a deeply inflicted wound caused by
someone who said they loved me. Nancy Leigh De-
Moss is right when she says that the clock can stop in a person's life when they continue to replay the hurt in their mind's
eye. She's also correct when she notes that hitting "replay"
in our hearts and minds allows us to almost see and feel the

actual surroundings where the injury took place. This shows how powerful our memories and our thoughts are when we choose to remember and replay them as well as why we need to take every thought captive (2 Corinthians 10:5), bringing these remembrances that are harmful to us and to others under the authority of Christ Jesus.

The Lord doesn't want us to remain chained to the blinding pain of betrayal and forever handcuffed to the particular memory. Jesus wants his followers to live freely. How do we break the heavy chains of painful memories of hurt caused by others, even those we call our friends? Through forgiveness. We must obey God and forgive others because he first forgave us (Ephesians 4:32). Forgiving someone, even a good friend, for something she didn't mean to do—or worse still, did mean—doesn't imply that the action wasn't wrong, or that we haven't forgiven our offender by simply remembering the event.

Forgiveness is a very different animal than forgetting. Thankfully, God created our minds to have recall, so we must choose to first use our will to forgive and then eventually the feelings will follow. If we want to honor God with our hearts and minds, then we have no choice but to pardon those who have sinned against us. The formula is this: Fully forgive = fully free.

Let's revisit the harder part of remembering a painful event at a most inopportune moment through a personal example. A friend of mine began acting out of character, or at least what I had assumed was her character. It troubled me greatly. I prayed fervently about how to best to talk through these "inconsistencies" (for lack of a better term) with her. We met, we talked, but we got nowhere. In fact, the whole conversation quickly made a turn for the worse when she began accusing me of totally unrelated negative repercussions being imposed on her because of her actions. In short, while my intention was to build a bridge of better understanding and hopefully offer some encouragement and trust between us, the conversation went in the opposite direction.

I remember leaving my friend, getting into my car, and feeling utterly shocked and blindsided. It took me a long time to fully work through my injured emotions and find peace in my heart about the situation. But first I had to forgive. Why? From my perspective, I was holding out hope for reconciliation that never happened. Second, I was at times tempted to replay the painful conversation when she accused me of harmful intent toward her. Whenever I started to hit the "replay" button, I began to discipline myself to say out loud specific Bible verses on forgiveness. That helped immensely. But in all honesty, even today, every so often I have to guard my heart and my thoughts that can so quickly turn to anger and bitterness over this event. I have to choose to forgive every single time that memory rears its ugly head—and by God's grace, I do.

When we, from a pure heart, truly desire to break free from the painful memories inflicted on us by others, even our friends, we have no choice but to offer in full measure forgiveness toward our offender. The truth is we cannot do this successfully without the enabling power of the Holy Spirit, who will infuse us with the grace to forgive and keep on forgiving when the painful memory pops up again. Certainly, it is much simpler to forgive a one-time offense. But how do we handle a friend who continues to sin against us in word and deed? How do we cope with the emotional pain that keeps recurring?

Most assuredly, we need to bathe these types of scenarios in prayer and seek out the wise counsel of other, more mature believers. We need to ask for wisdom and guidance to first of all address the sticky situation with insight and grace. Then we need to seek out practical ways to make the attempt to bridge the gap through careful, grace-infused conversation. Next, we need to leave the grievance in God's hands. If you have a similar situation, but in this case your friend desires reconciliation and peace, you can begin to rebuild your friendship (remembering, though, to place new boundaries that include mutual respect and selfless care for each other). Hopefully, broken relationships can be restored and even strengthened once time, trust, and the healing power of God blankets the entire friendship.

 Take-away Action Thought

No matter how much I hurt, I will seek to restore a broken relationship and I will begin by fully forgiving the one who offended me.

My Heart's Cry to You, O Lord

Father, help me to obey you by fully forgiving my friend who hurt me. I want to be free of these lingering painful memories that seem to pop up out of nowhere. Lord, give me your eternal perspective on forgiveness, and remind me that I need to forgive someone who injures me, whether it was intentional or not. Please, Holy Spirit, fill me with the grace to love unconditionally and remind me of my own sinful tendencies. Will you help me to communicate in a loving, humble, and grace-infused way to my friend so she is confident in my love for her? I can become fully free only when I forgive fully. Therefore, enable me to honor and obey you in this important matter. Amen.

Focus on Friendship

1. Today, seek to fully forgive any wrongs done against you and ask the Lord to build a bridge of full reconciliation and restoration in your friendship.

2. Right now, pray for your friend and ask the Lord to deepen your commitment to honor him by seeking forgiveness, and then the commitment to create the kind of biblical friendship he can bless.

3. Discipline your thoughts every day and don't allow yourself to hit the "replay" button on any perceived wrongs done against you. Instead, recite Scripture verses that focus on offering forgiveness.

 *Chapter 24*

Exhort and Encourage (Speak the Word of Truth Out Loud and Often)

The discerning heart seeks knowledge,
but the mouth of a fool feeds on folly.

Proverbs 15:14

*It is a heavy responsibility to know our theology benefits
or weakens others depending on what shape it is in. This
knowledge reinforces the urgency of pursuing a deeper
knowledge of God, wrestling with the truth and keeping
our eyes fixed on him. Knowing God keeps us focused on
what really matters, helps us steer a steady course through
troubled waters, and equips us to minister to others.*

Carolyn Custis James

I have always loved this quotation by Carolyn Custis James because it helps women to see the importance of understanding theology. In another one of her fabulous books, James writes that as soon as you ask the question "Why?" you pose a theological question. The how-to of gaining theological prowess begins by opening your Bible day after day and studying its contents. You have to know what God's word says about Jesus, the Holy Spirit, God the Father, and every principle required for living a life that honors him through the pages of Scripture. Whether you are searching for verses on relational woes, a healthy body and mind, death and life, the proper use of money, love or hate, kindness or jealousy, depression or joy—whatever wisdom you need—the Bible supplies.

In my darkest times when my emotional pain was threatening to overtake what I knew to be true about the faithfulness of God, my friends who are students of God's word helped me the most. It's not that others can't or aren't able to offer comfort; they can. For the Christ follower who has a personal relationship with Jesus, however, only God's word with its living, active power can deliver exactly what believers need in their times of personal crisis.

I've watched other friends, whose circumstances were so daunting and so overwhelming, begin to doubt God's love for them. They spiraled downward into depression and verbalized their confusion about God's plan for their lives. Enter in women who were strong in their theology, who knew what the Bible says about the unchanging character of God. Once they started sharing what the Bible says about God and his powerful love, my friends' confident proclamations that God will provide and make a way became highly contagious. Even those whose hearts were nearly breaking started to pay attention and were motivated to turn their hope and trust back to him. I have chills running down my spine as I recall some of these powerful moments when truth was shared—and yes, declared out loud—and the spiral downward into despair ended right then and there. Yes, theology matters.

Remember this: preparing for the unknown, the unexpected, and the unbelievable cannot wait. So what will you do today to start equipping your heart and mind for your next day of trouble? Or for the day of your friend's trouble? This is the day we all must invest time and energy becoming familiar with passages in the Bible that we can read when a sudden disaster hits us or our friends. How sad it is to wake up to a crisis and find yourself unprepared (emotionally, mentally, physically, or spiritually) for no good reason.

If you won't invest time getting into God's word for yourself daily, then do it for those you love. The next time one of your good friends calls and is crying (and crying out for help), you can be ready to answer. I'm not suggesting you flippantly read off a series of Bible verses to your hurting friend. Rather, listen carefully, pray all the while, and try to discern what the root of the problem truly is. Then, when your friend has poured out her heart, you can gently, quietly, and kindly offer her some key passages of Scripture that will provide her with a solid foundation for trusting God through her storm. You may reach out and share a few verses on combating worry and fear if that applies. Or perhaps bring out a passage on the importance of disciplining one's thoughts so that our emotions do not take control of our lives. The resources found in God's word are endless. But it doesn't do anyone any good unless someone (you and I) mine these nuggets of golden insight and wisdom ahead of time. Become a woman who is skilled in understanding theology. It matters to you. It matters to your friends.

Take-away Action Thought

I will dedicate a specific portion of my time to studying the Bible and then note any key passages I know will be of use to my friends or me during times of trouble.

My Heart's Cry to You, O Lord

Father, help me to take seriously the studying of your word so I may be equipped during my own times of trouble. Remind me, Lord, that my friends will thrive or sink due in part to my ability to offer them biblical exhortation and counsel. I need to see the importance of preparing in advance so I am not caught off guard or ignorant in the midst of a trial that threatens to undermine my faith. Help me internalize your unchanging character and be reminded of your promises to provide me with everything I need. Keep inspring me to seek more knowledge, and bring understanding to my heart and mind. Amen.

Focus on Friendship

1. Before you go to bed tonight, invest time into becoming a better, more skilled theologian. Seek out greater understanding of the tenets found throughout the pages of Scripture.
2. Invite your friends to do a Bible study and then work through each book of the Bible together.
3. When your friends are hurting and their faith is wavering, spend time locating passages of Scripture that will speak directly to their struggle, exhorting them to honor God by trusting him throughout the challenging circumstances.

 # Chapter 25

Envision a Positive Future (Remembering That with God Everything Is Possible)

Whoever seeks good finds favor,
but evil comes to one who searches for it.

Proverbs 11:27

Some things may legitimately be alleviated, others necessarily endured. May we be wise enough to know the difference.

Elisabeth Elliot

I am acquainted with a family, whom I see sometimes only every five years or so, who has been deeply hurt by the people in their lives. Hurt by their immediate and extended family. Hurt by their coworkers. Hurt by their local church. When you spend any amount of time with this family, you cannot help but like them! They are great people. They love the Lord. They are committed to doing what is right at home, work, and at play. On the surface they seem so easy to get along with.

Although I love this family deeply and commiserate with their multiple sets of awful circumstances, it has kept me wondering why these painful events keep happening to this particular family. So what's the rub? After having had a number of get-to-the-heart conversations with different members of this family, I've come to the conclusion that we can be "great people" but still be so broken and wounded that our lives continue to run amok. I'm not privy to what happens behind the scenes of their lives, but I can tell what these individuals have shared with me about their family's accumulated woes. Each of the members of the family admits to feeling defensive most of the time. That is, they are so afraid of being hurt again (as a family unit and individually) that they have taken on a harmful "us against them" mentality. And it shows.

On the surface, all looks well, and I've often marveled how this family has continued to rise up against their difficulties over the years. But of late, I'm seeing quite a different picture. They haven't risen above anything. They are reactors and not active in forging a healthier and biblical model for addressing pain. Unfortunately, the parents set the example for their children, and now the children emulate their parents' defensive attitudes and actions. All for what? To protect themselves from further injury and harm? To shield themselves from potential pain? To draw their family circle into a point of being impenetrable? This is no way to live. My hope and prayer is that someone, somehow, can break through their defensive maneuvers long enough to show them a different, more courageous way to live despite the pain they have experienced. As of right now, they aren't living; they're merely existing.

Of course, we can all agree that hardship and suffering comes to everyone. The specifics are unique to each of us, but the overall principle remains steady and sure. Life on a sinful, broken planet will necessarily mean that we all will be called on to face tragedy, injustice, and pain. How we choose to deal with the worst life has to offer us is where we must concentrate our efforts. Our attitude about suffering (our own in particular) will reveal what we believe about God, about the principles found in Scripture, and about our personal relationship with Jesus.

There is so much wisdom and good sense found in Proverbs 11:27 cited above: "Whoever seeks good finds favor, but evil comes to one who searches for it." A quick review of the previous chapter about the importance of being good theologians needs to be revisited here. Using the family depicted above as the perfect example, how might this group of individuals overcome their past seasons of suffering and trials? Certainly not by hunkering down in defense mode where fear governs their every thought and action. Instead, consider how very different this family's life (and potential ministry) might look if they realized that God was far bigger than anything they have to endure.

When I feel like I'm in a season where enduring a trial is the goal rather than thriving in spite of it, I need to remind myself that something is off. When God wants to teach me something that will transform me more into Christ's likeness, I need to be teachable. Rather than doing my level best to escape the teaching moment (and the related emotional pain), my response should be, "Lord, what do you want me to learn from this experience?" As I discipline myself to respond to life's difficult moments in this way, I often circumvent God's need to up the ante by getting my attention in stronger (and occasionally more painful) ways.

We are all on the bus of life, and if we don't accept God's lessons (in the guise of hardship/suffering/pain) the first time around, he keeps us circling the same route until we get it. The bus route gets longer, more uncomfortable, steeper, and unpleasant. Why? God wants our attention. One way or another, he will fulfill his purpose in our lives. Let's be wise enough to humbly submit to God's instructions and help our friends get off their bus rides.

 Take-away Action Thought

I will humbly accept the unwanted hardships in my life as God's tool of instruction to conform me into the image of Christ.

My Heart's Cry to You, O Lord

Father, help me to be a teachable, humble woman of faith. Give me the wisdom to respond to personal pain and disappointment by turning directly to you. Although I am confident in your perfect love for me, there are events so painful that I want to run from them. Give me the courage to face my fears, knowing you will do a good work in my heart and mind. If I need to endure hardship for a season or more, give me the staying power to prevail over my trials. Help me to be the kind of friend who rightly counsels those who are suffering to return to you. Give me the right words to provide renewed hope and trust in your plan for my friends' lives. Create in us all tender, teachable, and trusting hearts. Amen.

Focus on Friendship

1. Right now, purpose to respond to hardship and suffering in your own life by immediately turning to God in prayer and by studying those passages in Scripture that proclaim his faithfulness and unconditional love for you.

2. Point your hurting friends to God's loving heart and gently remind them that he has promised to meet their every need. Then do what you can to support and encourage their hearts along the way.

3. If you begin to get bitter or angry with God for what he is allowing in your life (or one of my friend's), call a friend you are confident can remind you of God's greater purpose in our lives.

 *Chapter 26*

*Stand Together During Times of Trouble
(Have Your Friend's Back at All Times)*

The righteous eat to their hearts' content,
but the stomach of the wicked goes hungry.

Proverbs 13:25

*It isn't easy to live in a fallen broken world where we hurt
and neither God nor life always make a lot of sense. But one
thing is sure. Whether we are in pain ourselves, or grieving
over the sufferings of others, we all live out our theology.
Either we will live under a cloud of despair, believing that
God has abandoned us, that for a moment we were out of
his hands and in the hands of fate or the devil, that we were
mistaken when we thought he loved us, that others are more
important than we are, or that his power simply doesn't reach
this far. Or we will live with hope, even in the midst of pain,
knowing that a good and loving God has marked out the race
we are running. He has done it for our good and his glory.*

Carolyn Custis James

*M*any years and dollars ago, we invested what was to us a large sum of money for our children's future college expenses. Since we had our four children within a six-year span, we were conscious of getting an early start as we anticipated future educational costs. Within a few months' time, however, our investor alerted everyone who had placed their money with him that the funds had been stolen by a couple of fraudulent employees. It was a shock and heartbreak to us who were living on a single income, and that investment forced us to start all over again.

As much as we were dismayed, our newly widowed friend had invested the entirety of her late spouse's life insurance with the same company. In one swift illegal move, her savings account (and her monetary security) was wiped out. As you can imagine, our friend was far more upset (and rightly so) than we were about our comparably miniscule loss. As time went on, we worked through our loss and disappointment (even with God) over what he had allowed. But our thoughts were never far from what we knew our widowed friend was enduring. Her life as she had known it was entirely upended.

Over time, she slowly worked through the emotional distress, placing herself completely into the care of the Lord. Eventually, she opened her own business—an elderly caregiving service—which would in time serve and minister to many seniors in our area. Our friend is doing well today from every perspective, so does the end justify the means? Did God have to allow our friend to lose her money in order to show himself strong on her behalf? Did he choose to let her go into a freefall financially so she would have to trust him completely? I cannot answer these questions. I can, however, testify to how God faithfully met her every need, and how she deepened and matured through this hard experience. God indeed marked my friend out for her particular race, and she won.

Standing with a friend who is in trouble is a sure sign of a lasting friendship. Casual friends may come and go—some may actually run away from a suffering friend. But friends who understand the biblical meaning of being a friend who is like Jesus—always faithful, always there for you, always supporting, encouraging, and exhorting when necessary—are priceless. As I reflect on the financial loss we endured long ago, I remember having a little wrestling match with the Lord at the time. I recall asking him, Why us? Then I had to willingly—with good grace and humble obedience—submit to his perfect plan for us. The lesson I learned through the experience was a deepening trust that the Lord would provide for us; the earth and everything on it is his anyway and that I needed to learn to be content whether we had a lot or a little. Those lessons have served me well over the years.

I also reflected upon what our widowed friend endured when her "safety net" of insurance money went to zero. She had recently lost her beloved spouse of many years, so she was still grieving and trying to figure out her new "normal." Then she believed she was wisely investing with a friend we all trusted (and still do), but the unforeseen happened and the money was stolen. There is absolutely no comparison between our meager suffering and her immense suffering. Still, when I talked with her about it, she had to go through the very same steps I went through with the Lord. She admitted to having lots of tussles with God over the event before she eventually chose to submit, trust, and move on.

We had good friends who helped us see the big picture, and so did our friend. Some of these excellent faithful folks ministered to both of us at the same time. They reminded us of God's sovereignty: that he never wastes pain; that he is always working to transform us into the image of his beloved Son; that he promises to make a way when there is no human solution; and that he gives grace, strength, hope, and help as needed. Our friends couldn't replace our money, but they offered us spiritual counsel worth its weight in gold. God had indeed marked our race in this particular way—and we now can all say that we won.

 ### Take-away Action Thought

I will place my hope and my trust in the Lord no matter my circumstances or my losses, because I know that the earth is God's and everything in it belongs to him.

My Heart's Cry to You, O Lord

Father, I am in great distress over the losses that have occurred in my life. I want to trust you through this crisis, but I'm not sure I have the faith for it. Help me to lean into your faithful arms, and surround me with your supernatural peace. Fill me with grace, hope, and the stamina required to endure whatever is coming. Thank you for wise friends who minister to me. Give me your eternal perspective, and keep reminding me that everything you allow is for my good and your glory. Be glorified through this situation! Help me to see how you are working behind the scenes to transform what I see as a tragedy into a triumph. Amen.

Focus on Friendship

1. Purpose to turn your troubled and shattered heart to the Lord before you turn to others for their wisdom and insights. Allow the Holy Spirit to minister his comfort to you before you look for friends and family to support you.

2. Pray first and foremost for any hurting friends to view tragedies through the lens of eternity. Ask the Holy Spirit to minister deeply to your friends and to bring supernatural comfort to their hearts.

3. This day and every day, keep your daily accounts clean before the Lord and don't allow yourself to linger in faithless or hopeless thinking. Rather, immerse yourself in the promises of Scripture that will strengthen your heart and resolve to trust God with everything that happens to you.

 *Chapter 27*

Serve Together
(Mesh Your Individual Giftedness)

Honor her for all that her hands have done,
and let her works bring her praise at the city gate.

Proverbs 31:31

*It's as though God has given each of us a song to sing, and
he is the choir director. He motions when it's time to sound
our notes and when to keep silent. He knows exactly how the
song needs to be sung. We don't want to make the mistake
of repenting of the song itself. He lays desires and longings
on our hearts. The song, then, is what we sing to his glory.*

Paula Rinehart

I have a friend I've known since I was five years old and she
was seven. We were first neighbors, and then we became
friends. When you share a friendship that literally spans
the decades of your life, you experience history (yours, hers,
and the world's) in the making. There isn't much we haven't
tried or experienced together over the years. We've had loads
of fun and laughter, as well as tears, sorrow, grief, and bitter
disappointment. But perhaps the very finest memories I have

of all the various events and life experiences we've shared is a brief season when we led a women's small group.

Over the course of a few years' time, we held these small groups in churches, at homes, and even at the local McDonald's! What I remember (and treasure) most about these women's group meetings was being able to observe God doing his transformational work in the lives of everyone who attended. It was exciting to gather week after week and open our selected text, work through it chapter by chapter, wrestle with truths that are difficult to understand (or accept), and then try to make them come alive in our lives. Story after story of how God revealed himself to each of us became the highlight of our weekly meetings.

For me, working alongside my closest lifelong friend was the icing on the cake. Together, we explored the principles of discipleship in Scripture, and then as a group we thoroughly discussed how these tenets can and should change us from the inside out. Having the opportunity to watch firsthand as God displayed his supernatural ability to change lives was tremendous, and having my friend share those experiences was a blessing and an excellent gift from our heavenly Father.

The Bible says that each of us has at least one spiritual gift, which means that each of our friends also has at least one spiritual gift. Churches and many parachurch organizations offer online character/gift tests for individuals to take and then determine where they are most gifted and how their talents might be best used in the local church and in life. If you have never taken one of these tests, ask your pastoral staff for references. Then take the time to work through the questions and evaluate the results. Encourage your friends to do the same.

Even better, invite your friends over one afternoon and with a computer (or whatever technology you use!), take the test and discuss the results as a group.

There is something about seeing the results of a test like this that can light a fire in a woman's heart to get busy using her gifts. The evidence of our gifts is revealed, and so excuses become feeble. Once you get a handle on the areas where you are most gifted, take some time to reflect on your life as it pertains to prior service opportunities and vocational experiences. Were there specific jobs or volunteer experiences that just felt wrong to you? Were there others when you knew you were exactly where you should be? Do friends sometimes comment on your ability to make a difference when you use your gifts? Do other moments feel forced or overly difficult for you? Take these feelings as cues as you prayerfully determine what's next in your life.

If you want to feel especially effective and blessed in any ministry opportunity, you should invite your women friends to serve alongside you. Remembering how each friend is uniquely gifted, try to position each one in her "sweet spot" of ministry. Then watch and see how God does his amazing work of transforming your life and your friends', and how you become part of a supernatural synergy that can alter the lives of everyone involved. Serving alongside friends is truly a gift, a very good gift from our heavenly Father.

 Take-away Action Thought

I will take the time to thoroughly understand how God has gifted me, and I'll encourage my friends to do the same.

My Heart's Cry to You, O Lord

Father, help me to understand the importance of discovering where you have gifted me. I tend to neglect this whole area of my life, but you created me for a specific purpose and part of that purpose is to strengthen my local church body. I cannot fulfill that purpose if I fail to understand where I fit in. Give me the needed insight and wisdom to determine my gifts, and then help me encourage my friends to learn what theirs are as well. I know firsthand the blessing of serving effectively with a good friend, and I'd love for all the women I know to experience that same joy. Open the doors of opportunity to us, and help us to walk through them as you lead. Amen.

Focus on Friendship

1. If you have not already done so, investigate the tests offered that will help you discover where you are most gifted.

2. Invite your friends to take this test with you and discuss your findings as a group.

3. Explore new volunteer and service opportunities, keeping in mind what you've just discovered about your gifts; be on the lookout for good matches for your friends as well.

 *Chapter 28*

Celebrate Together
(Rejoice When Your Friend Rejoices)

A generous person will prosper;
whoever refreshes others will be refreshed.

Proverbs 11:25

The common theme that emerges from the lives of women
who smile at the future—women who love their lives—
is that they've discovered the intersection where their
deep gladness and the world's deep hunger meet.

Paula Rinehart

I remember the day a single mom friend went back to college to finish her bachelor's degree, and I rejoiced. I recall this same mother of three completing her master's degree just a few years after that, and I rejoiced again. I think back to another friend who struggled for years to find the right vocational fit, and when she did we rejoiced. Yet another friend received a scary medical condition—one she fought long and hard—but today she is healthy again, and I rejoice.

Every time a new idea for a book fills my heart and mind, and then months or even years later it is published, my friends rejoice. Whenever I'm able to get my articles into a magazine I've been trying to break into (which sometimes takes years), my friends rejoice. When I finish up any interview (radio/TV/print), my friends rejoice.

It is exactly as Paula Rinehart states above. When you meet women who can smile at the future and love their lives, it is because they have discovered that intersection where—as Frederick Buechner famously writes in *Wishful Thinking*—their deep gladness and the world's deep hunger meets. It's true. I meet women who often bemoan their circumstances and whine about this or that. In all honesty, I want to run away from them. Then there are those women who have faced down obstacles greater than I have ever known, and yet they smile at me (and at the future). They are amazing, and I want what they have to rub off on me!

Just as Rinehart has noted through her counseling and writing career, often those winsome, joyous women have overcome the worst and live to rejoice in the best. Consider your own interactions with the females in your circle, and ask yourself which camp these friends fall into? Moaners? Whiners? Or overcomers who smile at the future and rejoice over what God has done for them and in them? Which camp do you want to be a part of?

I know a woman who is in the middle of a quandary. She recently started going to a gym in the wee hours of the morning (while her family still sleeps) to work out. She then rushes back home and showers, gets ready for her work week, feeds her family, and sends them off to their respective places of employment or school. Over a period of a few months, my friend's outward transformation has been startling. She always looked fine to me but now, wow! She looks like a real athlete because she is one now. Every time I see her, I rejoice.

My friend tells me that the daily discipline it's taken to rise early, get to the gym, work out, and then greet a full day of responsibilities has changed her for the good. She says the benefits of regular exercise have strengthened her physical body for sure. But that is only the beginning. Her mind is clearer, her memory is sharper, and perhaps most important, her resolve to overcome challenges that once sent her running for the hills now has her facing her fears head on.

But sadly, given all the excellent reasons for working out that are clearly evident to anyone who knows my friend, some folks still try to sabotage her with cutting, cruel, and critical remarks. Believe it or not, some of her friends question her priorities, the time she spends working out, the monetary cost, and—get this—her motivation. Some misguided individuals have actually suggested that all my friend cares about now is how she looks. It's pretty stunning that anyone who calls herself a friend of another woman would undermine her efforts to be strong in her mind and body.

I share that sad story for one reason only: to remind us all to be the kind of friend who celebrates with our friends who work hard to reach their goals. Rejoice with them when they have good reason to rejoice. Applaud their efforts, and encourage them by offering generous words of support. Refresh them with your admiration. Do it with a heart full of rejoicing, full of joy.

Take-away Action Thought

I will rejoice with my friends when they reach the goals they set out to accomplish. I will celebrate with them along the way by encouraging them in all the ways I can.

My Heart's Cry to You, O Lord

Father, give me a generous heart that truly loves to rejoice with others who accomplish their goals. Help me to be encouraging and supportive in word and deed. Never let me become a stingy woman who views other women's successes as a competition between us. Lord, each of us has a different road to travel through life, and each of us has to face down our own specific set of obstacles. I want to be the kind of faith-driven woman who overcomes my own struggles and then helps others do the same. Give us all the wisdom to know how to bring the right kind of encouragement to those friends who are still trying to find a reason to smile at the future. Amen.

Focus on Friendship

1. Rejoice with any of your friends who are working hard to succeed in an area of life that matters to them. Find ways to lighten their loads in practical ways too.
2. Pray for your friends to have the stamina to keep going, even when the pressures of life push back and they begin to wonder if their efforts will ever pay off.
3. Intend to be that kind of woman who smiles at the future, because you are confident that God has orchestrated your path and wants to use you to build his kingdom.

 # Chapter 29

Heal from the Past
(Listen, Pray, Support, Counsel)

Listen, my [daughter], to your father's instruction
and do not forsake your mother's teaching.
They are a garland to grace your head
and a chain to adorn your neck.

Proverbs 1:8–9

*Jesus wanted Mary to learn because he knew how desperately
she and other women would need it—not just for the terrible
shock of first grief but for the long road ahead (Luke 10:42).
When the bottom dropped out of her life and she was in a
freefall, what she knew of Jesus would be all she had to
hold her up. Knowing him wouldn't spare her from pain
and suffering, or even from disappointment, confusion, and
grief. But it would give her hope in the darkest moments and
a pervasive sense of purpose in the most confusing times.*

Carolyn Custis James

"M e too." As we saw in an earlier chapter, this is
sometimes the best thing we can say or hear in
trying to offer or find comfort and sympathy (or in

this case, empathy). In this chapter, we will look at how these two words might possibly be the two most important words you can say in answer to a grieving, pain-stricken, depressed, and downtrodden friend. I am confident that one of Satan's cleverest, most devious tricks is deceiving women into believing that their set of circumstances, their particular private history, their portion of pain, is unique to them. The enemy wants nothing more than to have us believe that we are the only ones who have experienced this kind of loss or depth of suffering. But it isn't so.

We have talked about what happens when one woman in a group has the courage to speak honestly about what she is struggling with—it may be her past, or her present, or the unknown future. Details are not the main point. The issue here is to tell a trusted someone (who shares your faith in Jesus) what has happened to you, what is going on right now, or what you fear most about the future given your past. We can heal only when we step out in faith with another mature Christ follower who is willing to listen to us, pray for us, support us as needed, and counsel us through the wisdom found in the Bible.

I have a friend who was abused by her stepfather during her elementary and junior high school years. She tried telling her mother what was happening, but her mom's own wounded brokenness wouldn't let her believe it. My friend's mother accused her of lying, which just layered pain on more pain. My friend began spending nights and days at another friend's home through high school until she graduated. She was smart enough to take steps to protect herself from her predator. But she will tell you today that she should have done more. She wishes she had gone to the police, her school counselor, or her pastor—anyone in authority who could have done more than her mother had done (which was worse than nothing).

Looking back, my friend doesn't judge herself; she understands that she was a young teen who took what she believed was the safest way out of a dangerous situation. But years later, after she became a mother, my friend was rather shocked when a whole new set of fears suddenly materialized. Wise woman that she is, she asked for counsel, support, prayer, and a listening ear from her closest friends. They didn't let her down. My friend needed most to connect with other women who had been through similar situations and who could say to her, "Me too." And they did.

If you, like my friend, have been traumatized (for any reason) in your past but haven't dealt with the betrayal, the pain, the suffering, or the memories, please seek out a trusted mature Christ follower who can help you heal. I have read and reread the passage found in Luke 10:12 where Jesus commends Mary for choosing what is better. I've puzzled over that verse more times than I can count. When I first came across Carolyn Custis James's explanation of how important it is to seek Jesus before we face tragedies (if we can), I was taken aback. I always assumed Jesus was simply admonishing Martha for not seeing the forest for the trees—meaning, why would anyone be preoccupied getting dinner together if Jesus was in the living room?

The more I considered Jesus' words to Martha, it became all the more apparent that he was encouraging her to seek him today because he knew what heartache and loss they would be facing in their tomorrow. For me, it was a lightbulb moment! Just as Jesus exhorted Martha to seek him above all else (work or play), he is telling us to do the same because he knows what we will be facing in the days to come. Jesus wants us to be prepared to lend a strong arm of support to our fellow sisters who are trying to make sense of their past, present, and future.

The point is we all need to hunker down and get serious about knowing who Jesus is and who he will be for us in our own seasons of dark sorrow. Help yourself heal from the past. Help your friends to heal from their pasts. Listen. Pray. Support. Counsel.

 Take-away Action Thought

I will heed Jesus' words to put first things first. I will spend time in God's word each day, studying to show myself approved in all things related to faith in him.

My Heart's Cry to You, O Lord

Father, my prayer is twofold. I desperately need to spend more time studying the Scriptures than I have of late. I've been busy, distracted, and, honestly, often distressed. I realize, however, that the more I invest in studying and meditating on your word of truth, the more my whole perspective is calmer. May the Holy Spirit nudge me daily to remind me of this fact. Help me also to be sensitive to my friends who are struggling to heal from their pasts. Give me your divine wisdom and insight as I offer them a listening ear, a commitment to pray, a hand of support, and words of counsel. Above all, help me to effectively communicate to my friend the importance of seeking you and making that the priority of their day. Amen.

Focus on Friendship

1. Seek to spend more time studying God's word and meditating on his promises to bring healing and restoration to your heart and soul.

2. Direct your hurting friends to Bible verses that speak of God's ability and desire to heal their past pain and to give them a bright future.

3. If you have pain in your own life that you have not dealt with thoroughly, then seek out a wise, mature Christ-following friend to help you work through the lingering painful emotions.

 # Chapter 30

Covenant to Go the Distance (Wherever That Takes You)

Blessed is the one who is kind to the needy.
Proverbs 14:21b

I've learned that the hardest things in life are those most worth doing—whether it's doing what others won't do, what you are gifted to do, or what you're feeling called by God to do. There's a big, broken world out there waiting for your neighborly love. My prayer is for you to walk across the street, yard, sanctuary, hallway, or office—wherever God's calling—and be bold, brave, and generous with your love.
Sarah Beckman

A good friend gave me an unexpected gift when I was getting ready for my fourth shoulder surgery. I was somewhat weary and quite apprehensive. I was also in a lot of pain and felt desperate to have my shoulder corrected. My friend, who had prayed me through the previous three surgeries, had noticed my growing anxiety and so she handed me a lovely book by Max Lucado. I remember reading this book in one hand while my other hand was in a sling. It lifted my heart. There's a reason why folks call Max America's storyteller. One of the devotions focuses on the value of loving friends and family, and the gist of the story is this: If you care about the people in your life, you show up for them. It's as simple as that. There's no fanfare or complicated hoopla required. You just show up. At the dinner table. At the ballpark. At a birthday party. At a funeral.

All this showing up stresses the importance of showing up at key life (and death) junctures. Our friends may not ask us to share in their sorrow when they say goodbye to a relative, but they will certainly appreciate our quiet presence among their immediate family and friends. Our friends may not think to impose on our already hectic schedule when they are recovering from a surgery or a lengthy debilitating illness, but they also won't tell us to go away if we bring a meal for their family. True friends go the distance for those they love, no matter what the situation warrants. They don't wait for a formal invitation or a gold-inscribed announcement. Even when it feels scary, covenant friends happily step in and serve their friends. They show up.

There's no doubt that the world we live in needs the love of Jesus. There's no arguing away the dire straits where people long for someone to serve them in neighborly love. If you're not serving your friends because you're aware of others who are closer to the situation than you but they aren't stepping up, then it's up to you to do so. Many, if not most, won't go into situations that make them feel uncomfortable. Look around and see who needs help or what needs doing. Then just show up.

For the woman who has made a covenant in her heart to actively love the people God places in her path, some of whom she calls friends, comparing your actions to what others are doing is simply wrong. Let God deal with all those people who should be stepping out of their comfort zone and stepping in to offer assistance. Perhaps God in his mercy and compassion has gifted you with exactly what your friend needs most. Then your calling is pretty clear: Go the distance no matter where that takes you. To the hospital. To a hospice. To a funeral home. To a women's shelter. To a psychiatric facility. To the grocery store. To a neighbor's house. Step up and step in to make a difference and make Jesus' presence known. Just show up.

 Take-away Action Thought

I will not allow unfamiliarity or the lack of confidence to stop me from serving a friend when the Holy Spirit nudges me. I will show up even when my knees are knocking and my hands are trembling.

My Heart's Cry to You, O Lord

Father, I never want the excuse that I'm not comfortable with entering into an unfamiliar situation to stop me from meeting a friend's need. I know that if you call me to serve someone, even when I don't know that person intimately, then you will provide me with the strength and grace to be a blessing. I want to be a woman who sees a need and steps in. Help me to be sensitive to the people you place in my path. Give me creative ideas and the right words to say when I'm with those who are suffering. Help me to remember that you have not given us a spirit of fear but of power, love, and sound mind (2 Timothy 1:7). I fully rely on you to bring hope, help, and comfort to those who need it today. Amen.

Focus on Friendship

1. Pray for the boldness, bravery, and a heart of generosity to enter even the most unfamiliar situations, ready to serve your friends.
2. Don't give in to worry, fear, or feelings of inadequacy, because God's word tells you that you can do all things through Christ who gives you strength.
3. When your friends are in trouble, remember the heart covenant you made to be faithful to them until your last breath.

Sources for Quotations

1. Nancy DeMoss Wolgemuth, *Adorned* (Chicago: Moody Publishers, 2017), 20.

2. Wolgemuth, *Adorned*, 37.

3. Sheila Walsh, *In the Middle of the Mess* (Nashville: Nelson, 2017), 65.

4. Lou Priolo, *Pleasing People*, (Phillipsburg, NJ: P & R Publishing, 2007), 123.

5. Paula Rinehart, *Better Than My Dreams* (Nashville: Nelson, 2007), 84.

6. Rinehart, *Better Than My Dreams*, 178.

7. Tim Lane and Paul Tripp, *Relationships: A Mess Worth Making* (Glenside, PA: New Growth Press, 2006), 40.

8. Lane and Tripp, *Relationships*, 11.

9. Nancy Leigh DeMoss, *Choosing Forgiveness* (Chicago: Moody Publishers, 2008), 182.

10. Max Lucado, *Everyday Blessings* (Nashville: Nelson, 2004), 260.

11. David Jeremiah, *Journey: Moments of Guidance in the Presence of God* (New York: FaithWords, 2012), 314.

12. Sarah Beckman, *Alongside* (New York: Morgan James, 2017), 7.

13. Lucado, *Everyday Blessings*, 263.

14. Randy Alcorn, *90 Days of God's Goodness* (Colorado Springs: Multnomah, 2011), 21.

15. Beckman, *Alongside*, 172–73.

16. Beckman, *Alongside*, 80.

17. Rinehart, *Better Than My Dreams*, 85.

18. Rinehart, *Better Than My Dreams*, 144–45.

19. Oswald Chambers, *My Utmost of His Highest* (Grand Rapids: Discovery House, 1992), September entry.

20. Beckman, *Alongside*, 155.

21. Paula Rinehart, *Strong Women, Soft Hearts* (Nashville: Nelson, 2001), 17.

22. Elisabeth Elliot, *Secure in the Everlasting Arms* (Grand Rapids: Revell, 2002), 147.

23. DeMoss, *Choosing Forgiveness*, 27.

24. Carolyn Custis James, *When Life and Beliefs Collide* (Grand Rapids: Zondervan, 2001), 198.

25. Elliot, *Secure in the Everlasting Arms*, 76.

26. James, *When Life and Beliefs Collide*, 116–17.

27. Rinehart, *Strong Women, Soft Hearts*, 25.

28. Rinehart, *Better Than My Dreams*, 160.

29. James, *When Life and Beliefs Collide*, 116.

30. Beckman, *Alongside*, 207–8.